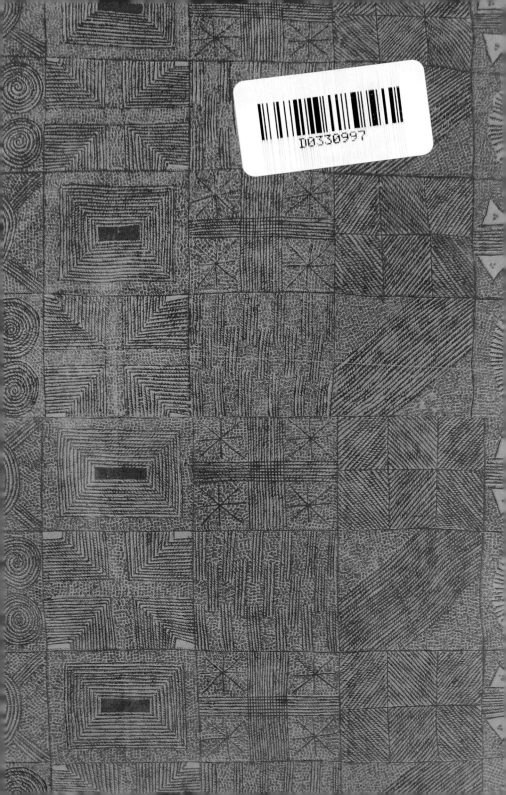

# indigo

# indigo

## IN SEARCH OF THE COLOR
## THAT SEDUCED THE WORLD

CATHERINE E. McKINLEY

BLOOMSBURY

NEW YORK · BERLIN · LONDON · SYDNEY

Published by Bloomsbury USA, New York

All papers used by Bloomsbury USA are natural, recyclable products made from wood grown in well-managed forests. The manufacturing processes conform to the environmental regulations of the country of origin.

LIBRARY OF CONGRESS CATALOGING-IN-PUBLICATION DATA
McKinley, Catherine E.
Indigo : in search of the color that seduced the world
/ Catherine E. McKinley.—1st U.S. ed.
p. cm.
Includes bibliographical references.
ISBN 978-1-60819-505-3
1. Indigo—Africa, West—History. 2. Textile fabrics—Africa, West—History. 3. Indigo industry—Africa, West—History. 4. Clothing and dress—Africa, West—History. 5. Africa, West—Civilization. 6. McKinley, Catherine E. I. Title.
GT1389.A358M35 2011
391.0966—dc22
2010046815

First U.S. edition 2011

1 3 5 7 9 10 8 6 4 2

Typeset by Hewer Text UK Ltd, Edinburgh
Printed in the U.S.A. by Quad/Graphics, Fairfield, Pennsylvania

For Shalom Oxana and Ephrem Blue

# CONTENTS

In ancient times, when the heavens hung closer to the earth, there was a woman who lived in the land through which the Niger River flows. One day she went to the river, and as she gazed at the waters and the reflection of the sky upon them, a hunger overcame her. She felt a great loneliness for God, who, tired of being whacked by the pestles of busy women, and wanting peace, had ascended up high. She felt too a hunger for beauty—beyond any beauty of the known world. She yearned for hair as blue as thunder, for cloth that was not simple white cotton. She wanted to become one with the sky!

Now in those times, bits of sky could be eaten. It was different from other foods. Rice fills the belly, but sky fills the heart. The woman reached for the sky and broke off a piece. But eating the sky could be dangerous business. One could become selfish in their desire, intoxicated, and this was a terrible taboo. The woman's hunger was stronger than her fear of what she knew had been forbidden, and she devoured more and more, until she was drunk with it.

As punishment, God pulled the sky higher.

With the heavens now so far above, and God even farther, the people of the land and their children, and their children for generations to come, each filled with their own great hunger, were set out on a trail of infinite desire. Their longing was made material in the bluest of God's blues—in garments dyed in indigo.

—Adapted by the author from West African folklore, various provenances

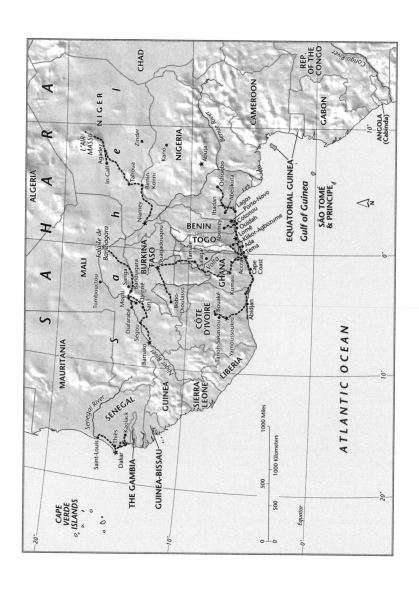

This book is a work of memoir and of historical narrative, but also a work of discovery—a piecing together of primary and secondary research, memory, impressions, interviews, and oral histories. The events are true; some details may have been altered to protect privacy. Any errors of fact are my own attempt to make sense of sometimes conflicting or competing records or claims. Some names, like those of Eurama and members of the Ghilchreist family, have been changed; most are of actual persons.

The term *obruni* appears throughout the text. It is a word that means, interchangeably, "white person" and "stranger" in Twi, one of the major languages of Ghana. Any non-African person is *obruni*, as is any African who is not a native speaker or has lived in or adopted a culture or manners of the West. *Obruni* has come to be used as a term of endearment. In postcolonial Ghana, in music and pop culture, and in the language of affection, it is often used without irony to mean "darling," "beloved," or "beautiful one."

Blue is one of nature's rarest colors. Indigo, a dye obtained from the tiny leaves of small parasitic shrubs that are part of the *Indigofererearsa* tribe, creates the bluest of blues. For almost five millennia, in every culture and every major religion, indigo has been one of the world's most valued pigments. No color has been prized so highly or for so long, or been at the center of such turbulent human encounters.

In the ancient trans-Saharan trade, whose peak extended from the eighth until the late sixteenth century, camel-powered desert ships carried indigo, along with African captives, gold, salt, kola, and other sumptuary items like ivory and ostrich feathers, to Mediterranean hubs where African, Arab, Asian, and European markets converged. Throughout the Middle Ages, Italians expanded this commerce across northern Europe, where it was in great demand for textile manufacturing because of its superiority to European woad in color, fastness, and fiber compatibility. For art and decorative architecture, indigo was a rare, refulgent, and costly material, used to express, as the contemporary Algerian artist Rachid Koraichi says, the "supraterrestrial . . . the path to the infinite." This idea was echoed in Christian, Islamic, and Jewish cultures, where it was used to symbolize the ancient caliphate, the royal court, the church and mosque, the canopy of heaven, a holy person's robes.

Indigo was used as a hair dye and an eye cosmetic in Europe; West African women rubbed it into their hair and skin, painted their bodies with it, and used it for tattooing and to enhance body cicatrization. It was burned as incense to ward off bad spirits. It was used as an antiseptic, a contraceptive, and an abortifacient; a cure for syphilis; and its root was regarded as a powerful sexual stimulant. Bodies were tattooed with it for healing purposes, particularly at the joints as relief from arthritis. Indigo tinctures are used for eye infections and as salves for wounds.

But as much as it was used for mysticism and healing and for beauty, West African women in particular wielded great social, political, and cosmological power as renowned master dyers and traders, and their indigo wealth became cornerstones of ancient empires and twentieth-century anticolonial movements, shaping the course of history and world economics.

For Europeans in the Middle Ages, indigo, referred to by some as "blue gold," had great value—and like chocolate and coffee and silks, it caught the imagination of connoisseurs, and merchants and colonialists, who drove a global market in search of the bluest blues. Because of the distance that had to be traveled to obtain the dyestuff, the strange and difficult alchemy necessary for its production, its power to bewitch, and its transcendent beauty, the value and demand for indigo became ungovernable. It threatened local woad production, sparked bitter trade wars, and touched off impassioned European and North American legislation and political debate. It became known as "The Devil's Dye."

After the collapse of indigo profits in the United States, India's production of indigo in the Rajshahi region was so lucrative that villagers were forced to harvest the plants by means of terror and torture. It was said that no indigo box was dispatched to England without being smeared in human blood, and resistance to that tyranny sparked a two-year peasant revolt—the Indigo Revolt of 1859— that Gandhi joined as his first civil action. The revolt brought a final end to the mass cultivation of indigo in the colonies.

Indigo was a cornerstone of the transatlantic slave trade—one of the hidden commodities, like cotton, sugar, salt, and gold, that fueled European colonial empires and compounded the extraordinary wealth and power of African ones. It grew wild along the southern coast of the United States. In the mid-1700s, Eliza Lucas, the sixteen-year-old daughter of a South Carolina plantation owner who was trained as a botanist, was given indigo seeds and soon discovered that her slaves had skill with indigo cultivation and indigo dye production. Aware that indigo was in great demand in European textile industries, coveted by gentry, soldiers, and workers alike, and that U.S. indigo would be cheaper than imports from Africa and Asia, Lucas convinced other planters to cultivate it. She is credited with introducing a crop more profitable than rice, which, because it had properties to repel the mosquitoes carrying malaria and yellow fever that caused the deaths of slaves—then two thirds of the population of the Carolinas—had inestimably higher returns. By the eve of the American Revolution, when cubes of indigo replaced paper currency, South Carolina planters were exporting 1.1 million pounds of indigo to Europe—nearly $30 million today.

The war would mark the beginning of the weakening of American indigo profits, also hastened by the invention of the cotton gin in 1974. The rapid industrialization of textile manufacturing that followed was spurred by that and earlier inventions like the spinning jenny and flying shuttle, water power, and Watt's steam engine, and the introduction of nonindigo synthetic blue dyes. Indigo's great profitability would altogether collapse by 1800, and the European hunger for indigo would turn to India, creating the conditions that led to the 1859 Indigo Revolt.

But indigo was not only the obsession of merchants and politicians and those seeking profit. The peculiar, magical alchemy of the indigo dye pot has dazzled and excited artists and scientists and thinkers alike. Sir Isaac Newton spoke of indigo as "visible yet immaterial," the color purest in meaning, with the power to negotiate the two spheres of God and man. Goethe's mention of it in *The Sorrows of Young Werther* incited a fashion craze, making it de rigueur for romantic young men to wear indigo coats over yellow pants in the 1780s. It inspired paintings by Bonnard and Matisse, who were both fascinated with indigo. Matisse famously used West African textiles, in which indigo figured greatly, as backdrops to many of his most significant portraits. And indigo has provided endless inspiration to American jazz and blues and the cultures they inspired.

This is just part of its little-known legacy.

I grew up at a seeming great distance from this history and from the African world, though both would become my obsession.

Raised in Attleboro, Massachusetts, a small factory town close to Providence, Rhode Island, I was a child of the 1960s: part of the post-segregation generation, born to a Jewish mother, the descendant of Russian and British textile factory owners, who was a student when she met my father, an African American and Choctaw Indian who was an artist and interior decorator in Boston. One of fewer than twelve thousand African-American children adopted transracially in the U.S. at the end of the segregation era, I was raised by Wasps in an all-white community. My adoptive parents, a high school history teacher and an engineer, were naturalists. My earliest memories are of long family treks—by kayak and canoe, on snowshoes and foot—into the wilderness. My parents seemed to seek extreme locations—places of great physical beauty that were difficult to reach. Plants and nature defined our world and, indeed, took over our house. Independence from others and a life of the mind were ideals.

From an early age, I felt myself in deep conflict with

my parents' desires for wilderness and solitude. Though I shared their love of beauty, I was searching for human connections. I was attracted to material culture, the things we live with, the beauty of the domestic (fashion and textiles), and I longed for people. The Cape Verdean-African community in Providence pointed to a tangible connection with Africa, and because we shared the appearance of the *métisse*—of being mixed race—for the first time my belonging was assumed. Somehow, these desires took root and Africa and design and storytelling became the things that defined me.

I left Attleboro to attend Sarah Lawrence College, where I studied creative writing. By graduation, I was on my way to join an Africana Studies department at an Ivy League university that, at that moment, was home to the most respected historians, philosophers, and writers on Africa and African America. My childhood unwittingly prepared me for what was ahead—my indigo journey. And by the time I arrived in grad school, and discovered that what African women wore were texts, history, and expressions of social identity—things with weight but also something playful and optimistic—I was freed to take it.

When I was a graduate student, studying postcolonial literature, I was dating a Nigerian professor who was much esteemed, considered by many a genius. His intellectual fire and political dissidence in Nigeria, at the university where he taught and as a trade union organizer, were legendary. He lived in a large, cold, somewhat remote house in upstate New York in self-exile—a bachelor's house, bare except for his books and only the most essential furniture. It struck me as the shelter of someone who did not accept the life he had made. Although it was full of comforts and privileges less tangible than a house and the material life he seemed to eschew, he seemed ashamed of his desire for them. It was the home of someone self-punishing. Its only soulful corner was a wall of his living room, where, high on the otherwise stark wood paneling, hung rare, beautiful indigo cloths, the hand-designed work of Yoruba women of Ibadan, the town where he was raised. The cloths were luminescent, ranging in intensity of color from powder to blue-black. Watching them was like moving through layers of sky.

I would get lost in those blues. They seemed to absorb the feelings of those who gathered in that house, recasting everyone in a kind of soulful beauty. The professor would often lie next to me, lost in his work and memories, and I wondered if the power of the cloth was what held me there, coloring his moody caress.

Long after I left school and my relationship with the professor ended, he stopped at my apartment in New York City en route from a visit to Nigeria. I was away and returned to find, at the foot of the bed, a small parcel wrapped in paper from a Lagos shop. As I peeled it away, a strong vegetal, smoky perfume opened my nose. After a few minutes the perfume gave way to an undernote of something urinelike but oddly pleasant. Inside was a cloth with tiny white hand-drawn batik designs—of abstract birds and reptiles and other animals, whose figures appeared more like handwriting—against a blue-black indigo background. The blue, and the scent, rushed my senses, and I remembered my feelings of pleasure and longing.

The cloth, like many indigo cloths, had a name, Ori mi pe, "My Head Is Correct." "You know, your *ori* is your soul, which is believed to reside in the head—your destiny. So this cloth means 'My destiny is good,'" he later told me. "I remember you always liked these things."

Each time I handled the cloth, it left ghostlike traces of blue on my hands, beautiful against the skin. They felt like a blessing or protection. I had moved to New York the year before hoping to begin a career as a writer, and was trying to make a home there amid the uncertainty and angst of my early twenties. I tried to preserve the stains, as if keeping that blue in my eye and on my hands was essential to preserving my balance, but they quickly faded, proving as elusive as his gesture.

Not long after I received the professor's gift, I traveled with two friends, a librarian and a painter, to Mali. We'd planned this somewhat impromptu journey over dinner, high from meeting the photographer Seydou Keïta at a SoHo gallery party, where his elegant, nearly life-size studio photos of Malian women and men in the 1950s were hung.

It was their first trip and my second; part of a pact to see all of West Africa before we were thirty, an age we'd assigned various vague and inhibiting responsibilities. One day after a long hike into the Bandiagara escarpment in Dogonland, we sat resting on a horse

cart at the foot of the cliffs. High above, blanched by the
atomic sun's glare, centuries-old mud dwellings nested in
massive rock shelves. I saw something moving in the cliff
tracks—a cool, brilliant, snaking band of blue, the color
as intense as the literal hum of the 104-degree heat of the
Sahel, the frontier to the Sahara.

Soon a group of Dogon women appeared. They wore
indigo skirts, inky dark, met at the waists by neon-bright,
boldly patterned demi-blouses, and huge, ornate amber
and gold jewelry. I was entranced with the riot of colors,
the dark tonal drama of brown and black skin mixing
with blue.

"They are sorceresses," our host explained. "You can
read their stories on their wrappers. They have come
from a women's gathering. Maybe there has been a birth."
I stared at the tiny white batik designs, like scarification
marks, and bright elliptical embroidery on the border of
their skirts.

As quickly as the women arrived, they moved word-
lessly past us on the trail, the sun again obliterating all
but the light from their skirts. I watched the retreating
band of blue, and a kind of welcome possession took over
as the eruption in my senses filtered into calm.

But later I felt flooded by a strange anxiety at the loss
of that beauty, at not being able to read those marks, and
at something else unnameable—a nearness to something
magical, or divine?—slipping out of my hands.

Learning to read and write is one of my most powerful,
even fantastical, childhood memories. As a child, writing
seemed to me like wizardry: the making of words, with

the exotic dark blue India ink (once made from indigo) that filled the fountain pens we used, seeming like a mystical source of my expression. I loved the print on book pages, newspaper ink, and the dark tattoo of the funny pages—it smelled pungent and rubbed off and stained, as if allowing the stories to live in you. I would chew the corners of the Sunday *Times*, forming small, hard tablets that I would swallow, associating those dyes with the power to speak and write. The Dogon women, wearing blue texts and signs, brought that sense of power and beauty back to me.

When those Dogon women parted, I too set off, like the woman of legend, on a path of unnavigated desire, in search of *ori* and my own blues.

In 1999 I began an overland journey, supported by a Fulbright grant, to search for indigo across nine West African countries, including Ghana, Ivory Coast, Mali, Burkina Faso, Niger, Benin, Togo, Nigeria, and Senegal. Indigo has profound spiritual and sartorial significance in most West African societies, and yet it has almost all but disappeared, replaced with less beautiful, synthetic blues and commercial imports, eroding the social and cosmological meaning of the sacred practice of dyeing. For much of this time I found myself wandering like a somnambulist, looking for something now rare, hidden from the uninitiated, difficult to enter; not always knowing what I was seeking.

I was accustomed to searching; it was as reflexive as my desire for indigo. As an adopted child, I had spent the ten previous years searching for family lost to me, piecing together the histories of several generations of Jewish "rag traders" who dealt in cloths, and descendants of African slaves traded along the same routes as indigo, where a length of blue cloth was a common exchange for human life. The naturalist parents who raised me were descendants of a clan of Scots who wore woad, or possibly indigo tartan as their virile armor. Their intense connection with the life of plants surely informed my own fascination with those small green African leaves. Indigo was in my blood.

I didn't fully understand, when I started on this four-year journey, that I was not just chasing beauty but trying to recapture some part of my own legacy and my blue inheritance. I was driven by a desire to live closely with that beauty; to become literate in the stories of those cloths; and to understand history through the African women, mostly, who mediate and wear and trade indigo. These women, unwittingly, taught me about birth and death and about the beauty and meaning that people make of the life space in between. They helped me to understand the power of these phenomena in my own experience and, as one of the heroines of my journey would promise, learn to truly "taste life."

# Part I

# SEEKERS

# one

# An Invitation, Ghana

It was a simple invitation. Voices from the tiny night market stalls—barely shelter, invisible in the rain-pounded, blackened street—called out, *Sorry-o! Sorry!* I stumbled past a row of shuttered stores hugging the gutter's edge, the wind fleeting my steps.

At a turn in the road, in the glow of a kerosene lamp, a woman cloaked in a dark sweater beckoned to me from under the canopy of a shop.

"Sister, you are no more at England. Come out of the rain!"

She looked hard into my eyes in a flash of lamplight. She grinned and pulled the sweater tighter against the curve of her face, ushered me inside, then disappeared through a back door into the night.

I felt a presence behind me. A stool was pressed against the back of my legs. And then a surprising heat: a wild orange and green spider's web-patterned wrapper—those essential two yards of cloth that West African women use as skirt or sarong or cover, baby carrier or headgear—dropped over my rain-soaked dress. A young woman at a sewing table giggled shyly as she put a charcoal-heated iron to the wrapper's mate. From the back of the shop, a girl emerged in a peacock-blue taffeta dress with heavy lace at the neck, worn and buttonless the length of its back. She shyly curtsied as she set a cup of tea before me. A bush dog, as large and white and nappy as a sheep, sleeping against a fortress of rice sacks, settled his head against my foot.

We sat in silence while the rain chorused against the tin roof.

It began to break in spurts, and I heard a clink of bottles and the slapping of leather slippers on the wet concrete. The woman reappeared, ferrying a stack of Coca-Cola crates on her head. She was petite, with a wasplike, near-Victorian waist, but she seemed more ample than small, with thick muscled legs and a belly curved by pregnancies. Moving swiftly, lithely, she lowered herself so the girl in the blue dress could relieve her of the load. She removed the scarf from her head, and her hair fell in a shiny black cascade of tiny braids framing high, kohl-dark cheeks and crescent eyes.

She fixed her smile on me, pulling wide the shutters on the shop doors.

People who had dug out army jackets, leather trenches, an oilcloth overcoat from closets buckled under equatorial heat, had begun to appear, crowding the entrance, dropping coins onto the table as they took away their purchases: a tiny cone of peanuts; a single teabag and two teaspoonfuls of sugar, one of milk powder, tied in plastic sleeves; a quarter or half bar of soap; a tin of sardines or corned beef.

I rose to leave, offering a *cedi* coin—pennies—for the tea. I was anxious to be home, to be away from the dangers of the flooded, unfinished roads.

"*Ei*, why? Even I brought this Coke to serve you," she said. "There is yam on the fire. Stay for some time! Someone can lead you home."

It was a familiar seduction. Invitations to sit, to eat, to be a sister or friend. The quick tuck of someone's hand in the street. Affection, sometimes gentle, sometimes groping. Accra *communitas*. "Accra is a society much more than it is a city," a friend had once observed. It is true— you can alight at any spot and "make yourself *akwaaba*." You are welcome everywhere.

The rain had begun to fall again. In the distance, flames danced along a wind-slackened electric power line that ran along the main sewer, an eight-foot gulf filled with months of rains.

I thanked her again, contemplating the footbridge to the gutter's other side.

"Take this jacket, to stay a little drier," she said. "You can return it anytime. I'm Eurama! Come back to us, eh? We'll make you happy-happy in Ghana!" I heard her sing as I stepped into the street.

The next day I set out in search of the shop at Nmetsobu Street with the jacket folded in my bag.

"You have come-o!" a familiar voice called from a perch at the shop door. "My lady has come!"

"I found something in the pocket of your jacket," I said, my heart racing. "It is real indigo!"

"*Ma ba?*" she laughed, quickly taking from me the tiny corner of cloth patterned like the Milky Way, tied around something hard and as long as a packet of chewing gum.

"You are very excited! Indigo. Yes. For me, it be money!"

She laughed a kind of outlaw laugh as she unwrapped it and a tight wad of *cedi* notes folded over a key. "Sit down and let me bring you tea. Don't rush! I have something I must do; I'll be with you very soon."

I accepted her offer of warm sugar bread and Lipton and ended up sitting for hours in the comfort of the canopy at the side of the shop. My mind stayed on that tiny bit of cloth.

My days had become like this—unstructured. Purposelessness was beginning to cloud them like the slow filtering haze from the early Harmattan, a season of powerful dry, dusty winds blowing from the Sahara toward the West African coast. I had been in Ghana for two months. Each morning I would set out from home with my bag, heavy with indigo research, but as the sun rose higher, my ambitions sagged. The university where I had set up base for my Fulbright work had been shut down by a strike. I'd exhausted the few small embassy libraries, filled mostly with trade and governance books. In the cloth markets and dyeing compounds, I'd met an indigo wasteland. Not a dyer or farm, not even the university botany lab, could produce one tiny *indigofera* leaf.

Here was a precious first scrap.

I waited for Eurama, watching the steady traffic of feet along the walls of stately former colonial residences, reclaimed family lands that now housed a mix of relatives of every social ilk, various African and Arab diplomatic corps, and Western expats. It was a grand crossroads theater. Across the street a young tailor sat working in a small wooden kiosk, smartly painted and fashioned with large glass windows that were expensive and mod. As the hours passed, fancy cars would stop at the roadside, and women would alight, handing their heavy designer purses to their drivers, aware of how they were admired from the street. They would then stand in that window for some minutes before the curtains would close so they could be measured and fitted. The shop window reminded me of Amsterdam's red-light district—the decorous promise and the thin veil between commerce and the street. Their cars competed for road space with women selling from head pans, wandering goats and sheep, and Ashanti boys pushing housewares or provisions arranged in wheelbarrows—their first step, after leaving home for the coast, toward a plane ticket to London or Italy or New York.

All the while my thoughts were with that bit of cloth.

When Eurama finally returned, she walked with a tiny box atop her head, a small handkerchief-size patch of the same indigo covering it.

From a bench at the roadside, in the same blue taffeta dress she'd worn the night before, Dede, her shopgirl, had been selling drinks to passing cars. Eurama stood, counted the coins in Dede's cup, and called playfully after people in the street with that flashing smile.

She saw me eyeing her head.

"Ah, this box be my wallet," she sighed, laughing. "You had my key-o!"

"I like the cloth," I said.

"This is part of a dress I wore when I delivered my last

child. I use it to keep my money safe, so that it will grow and so no one will covet it. Anyway, you can get some of this cloth." She shrugged. "I mean, you won't get it easily. It's an old design. But as it is almost the end of Ramadan, and Christmas too is coming, the Hausa people will be selling some. I can take you to them after the fasting."

She reached up to a shelf above and retrieved a sleeve of photographs. She handed one to me.

In a photo from the 1980s, Eurama stood in a studio, wearing a set of heavy gold jewelry and a blue-black damask boubou with a white pattern resembling the cosmos across the hem and her elaborate headgear. It was the same cloth that covered her box. She was proudly holding a bright-eyed newborn.

"It is proper-proper Guinea indigo."

The photo was just that—a photograph. Not the thing itself. Just a sign of a certain kind of understanding.

But it was all the hope I needed in a moment when my fortunes seemed to have turned against me. I had only just begun my work, but having a Fulbright grant suddenly seemed like a grand folly. I'd originally applied for a grant to Nigeria, but the political situation there was worsening and Fulbright grants were suspended. I was asked to make a case for Ghana, where indigo had been heavily traded but not much produced, and I put together an argument. But each day, as I turned up so little, the proposal seemed more and more hackneyed. I had just turned the corner of thirty. I'd left my job as a university administrator and creative writing teacher, given up my lease in the loft I shared in the East Village, and packed my things into storage. I knew almost no one in Ghana, though I'd traveled there before and had forged a few friendships.

It was the eve of Y2K, and the world was staring down rumored oblivion. "If America will collapse, how much Africa?" people bemoaned as they hoarded U.S. dollars. Ghana's currency plummeted daily, and people readied themselves for the coming departure from office of Flight Lieutenant Jerry John Rawlings, Ghana's maverick president for twenty-one years. I decided I'd sit out the uncertainty of the last days of the millennium and the regime in Eurama's comfortable store, hanging on to her promise to lead me to the indigo sellers.

In the weeks to come, my visits there would frame my days. After breakfast I would sit with Eurama and settle my ambitions on the Twi and Ga language guides she bought for me one day from a bookseller's head pan.

"You can't talk!" she had teased as she paid for them. "Of course you can't do anything in Ghana! I'll send you to Eurama University."

While I was in the shop, I kept the tiny books tucked inside a magazine, trying to follow the exchanges with customers.

"*Bloudo, enyi?*" How much is bread?

"*Ha mi omo kotoku kome.*" I want a bag of rice.

"*Paacho, sicle kitin kitin.*" Small sugar, please.

In the notebook where I copied down Twi and Ga phrases, I'd folded a favorite quote:

And I tell you, if you have the desire for knowledge and the power to give it physical expression, go out and explore . . . some will tell you that you are mad and nearly all will say, "What's the use?" For we are a nation of shopkeepers, and no shopkeeper will look at research that does not offer him a financial return within one year. And so you sledge nearly alone, but those with whom you will sledge will not be shop-keepers: that is worth a great deal. If you march your Winter Journeys you will have your reward, so long as all you want is a penguin's egg.

Apsley Cherry-Garrard,
*The Worst Journey in the World*

I was a shopgirl suddenly.

I tried to pitch in, to help with sweeping and stacking shelves, tying "ice water rubbers"—small plastic bags that Dede filled with tap water for drinking.

"Ah, sit down and relax," Eurama would insist.

"I can't just sit and be useless."

"My dear, never say that—you are good for business!" she said happily. "'The Stranger is God'—it is one of our sayings. Everyone wants to come and look at the *obruni*'s face. And then you are from New York—hei! The shop past the junction complained that I am taking all of their customers. You see, you don't need to do much to help out here!"

I'd become intoxicated in my post, and now I felt a little worried. I had hoped real affection guided their embrace of me and not something so mercenary.

"We like you! You remind us of my sister's daughter

who is in Washington. We are having some half-castes in our family. My sister married a British—he paid dowry and performed our marriage customs and everything! He had a big job with manganese. Then he was transferred to Sierra Leone. When my sister delivered, she packed her things and put the baby on her back and took a steamship all the way to Freetown. Heh! And met his London wife! But anyway, that is just a story. We like you fine! And I can see you need help with this your work."

And with that a true deal was struck: a funny kind of patronage for the newest shopgirl, in exchange for a promise and a kind of belonging.

I was fascinated by Eurama—by her beauty, her quick tongue, her stories, and the kind of mysterious power she wielded with people. The sudden ease of our agreement was fascinating too.

It was an act of volunteerism—becoming Eurama's darling. There was an innocence to it, a gamble, and a certain desperation too.

In the days that followed, at any hour, you might find me there, the Stranger God. Stacking a few tins. Sitting at the sewing table that her sister, Lady Diana, who had been named for the princess, worked upon. At the perch at the side of the shop. Standing at the roadside, Eurama's arm circling my waist.

"People's 'Rama!" neighbors called. "She's not only for you, *obruni*. She belongs to us all!"

"This is my darling!" Eurama would laugh.

"Aunty Eurama, I am also a human being. Come and hold me *small*!" they teased.

"Eurama Spider has caught a lovely something!"

*"Omo a wa hoye fe no ye nya ewo omo."*

" 'The beautiful ones are not yet born.' Hmmmm," she laughed. "It's a saying. You see, the thing you desire with all your heart—well, don't rush for it. Don't force. You will likely find that it is not the very thing you are looking for."

She seemed lost in thought, a kind of wistfulness moving in her.

*"Obruni,* be patient," she sighed. "You will get your indigo."

Eurama and I would sit on the bench in front of the shop for long hours watching the road, as she counted her tiny profits.

I would ask about indigo, my questions like those of a child. Her answers were like answers to a child's riddle.

I watched a woman passing, her high, shapely buttocks rolling beneath her skirt. "Why is she wearing blue?"

"Ahhh, maybe she's going to meet her boyfriend. Blue is the color of love. You see blue, it has its own smell, it even has a sound! It can be cool or hot—just like love."

I thought of my professor. That was cool love.

"Blues are God's stethoscope—they hold every feeling!"

"And she?" I asked. A woman stood at the gate of a house down the road, holding the hand of the old woman she had been visiting. She was wearing a blue and white factory-made batik with the spider print that seemed to be popular. The baby at her back appeared nested in the web. She had a small handbag balanced on her head, and an umbrella to shade them.

"She is a new mother. She has stayed indoors for the customary time. The baby is healthy, they've named it, performed the birth rites, and she is proud to show him to everyone. We wear blue for life!"

Later, a small band of women in long formal dresses all styled from the same white cloth with deep indigo batik flowering vines filed down the street, solemnly negotiating the gutter's edge.

"Why are they wearing blue?"

"Owụ Sē Fiẹ. You see-o!" Eurama sighed. " 'Death Spoils a House'—There Is Death—the cloth they are wearing tells us. They are from the baker's house. It will be the old lady. It is a good death. She was very old and had a good life. Blue is God's color. They are praising God for all that has been given. I will have to dress up this afternoon and go and sit with them."

Another day a middle-aged woman passed us. She walked trancelike, gazing into nothingness, her bare feet making quick, shuffling steps. Her head was shorn, and her bare breasts hung nearly to her waist. Long white beads hung over them and were fastened cufflike at her ankles and upper arms and wrists. Three strands of white beads were tightened against a dark blue cloth at her waist.

"And this woman? Is she after love?"

Eurama laughed. "She is a bush girl! Look at her breasts—hanging like empty socks! Here in Accra, we don't do that!" Eurama said. "This woman is Ewe, from the Volta region. She is from a shrine and probably married to a fetish priest. She's witchcraft. The blue is what the gods demand. Hummpf. Some of them take some herbs and behave like mad people. Maybe she's lost. She's going to follow the road along the ocean to find her way back east."

She clicked her tongue in disapproval and then playfully slapped my cheek.

"Or do you want to go with her? Your spirit also begs for blue. Blue-blue! It is all you think of. Go with her! It has already let you get up and leave your country, forget your family, forget everything!"

We watched the woman disappear into the bend of the road. It was unsettling. She seemed possessed, driven by some mimetic force. I was afraid that that force was also a part of me. I was also a worshiper, set wandering in an unfamiliar land.

"*Obruni*, I don't really understand *what exactly* it is that you're after. You are a writer? Uh-huhhhhnnnn." Her face knit slightly with worry. "You love indigo. You have a big scholarship from your embassy to make research. Fine! You say you have everything. A good career, a good life. It's only indigo you need. But how is it you are so alone? You are here in Ghana with only your Eurama. You say you don't have a lover, a child. Nothing. We are waiting for your family to come. Okay, you say your parents don't like to travel and leave their farm, but we are waiting for your American lover at least. You don't keep a cell phone; you hardly call anyone. Cloth is cloth. It is everything to us, and it is nothing. It only becomes part of a devotion to other things, to people. You have to start life! Have a child. Get married—at least marry to have a child! Make a home! Care for another human being and make one with them."

We sat for a long time in silence. I was surprised by her passion, by how she'd observed me. I let her plea roll over me. She had only known marriage and shopkeeping, hard menial work, domestic life, children. I was the freest woman in the world, living a life of the mind on an esteemed American artist grant. I was not bothered by my solo trek; I'd worked hard to live unencumbered. But her words had a strange power too. It was as if she'd pointed at something akimbo in me, as obvious to her as the odd stupor of the shrine woman.

"I need to do this work for now. There is still time to sort out those other things," I said, wanting to turn the conversation.

Eurama sighed. "Yes, madame. Be patient, then, and you will understand everything you need to."

Eurama began to invite me along to buy stock for her shop. Every third day I would awaken at dawn and accompany her to Makola, Accra's central market.

When we reached the market's edge, Eurama would grab my hand and say, "*Waatey!* Let's go!" Then we'd step into the acres of what appeared as a vast, gray, curiously undulating flatland from any station above its tin roofs. Inside was a dangerous crush of head loads: improbable portages of yams and car engines and bags of rice, nets filled with live chickens, calabashes of honey, stacks of plastic buckets, bolts of cloth, canned tomatoes, peanuts arranged on trays as if they were works from a modern design studio, crates of eggs, a tray of stinking pigs' feet or enormous forest snails for soup, and a shimmering globe of nail polish bottles arranged in a plastic bowl by a woman who would dress your toes at any place where you could find room to rest.

In the narrow passages moved *kayayo*, the mostly Muslim girls sent down from the north by their families. They sleep in bands in the market, and from dawn to dusk they carry spine-breaking loads to earn the capital for their marriage dowries. They work their way up to petty trading, with dreams of becoming store traders or even the fabled market queens—the cloth sellers at the top of that hierarchy—who control prices. Smaller agents and scores of petty traders scramble to raise themselves in the market hierarchy. Women and men passed me with Chinese Black Butterfly sewing machines on their heads, calling customers by snapping their long, heavy shears, adding to the din of shouts and car motors, competing radios, and the whir of tired refrigerator fans. Groups of petty traders editorialized the world of the market hierarchy by singing praise songs to their madames and insults to the Accra Metropolitan Authority guards who walked by barking orders and striking table legs and store sides with their punishing canes.

Eurama hired a *kayayo* to follow us as we bought what was needed to replenish the shop—pins and soaps and rice, biscuits, toilet paper, zippers, and buttons.

Once in the middle of this market there would have been an island of blue cloth. But that island slowly was swallowed up by the tall piles of mostly cheap factory-made cloths imported from China and India and Europe, and fewer uninspired tie-dye and batiks, "local cloth," made with synthetic dyes on cheap cottons. Bigger stores sold expensive imported laces and damasks and European-made prints, but these "local cloth" designs had a roteness: uninspired, they were the work not of master dyers but of young women and men in the stumbling technical school economy, exercising their narrow options of training in hairdressing, batik-making, sewing, or catering.

The cloth markets, vast as they were, were overwhelmed by the nearby sheds where bales of second-hand clothing were spread on the floors. Ghana had no full-scale ready-made clothing manufacturers, and the country seemed to have traded a large part of its sartorial brilliance, created from the explosive range of hand-tailored African cloths, for ship container loads of *obruni wawu* ("the white man has died"). Despite intermittent government bans to protect the enormous local cloth and tailoring industries, and health department campaign warnings, secondhand clothes from the United States and Europe had become a multimillion-dollar economy. Channeled mostly through Western charities, the clothes were graded and shipped and then resold across the African continent. Everyone loves a T-shirt, jeans, socks, and a sturdy bra, and so they defied the age-old notion that cloth is *spirit*—that a person's spirit, their ghost even, lives in their clothes—and bought them. *Obruni wawu* was the dominant attire at the cocoa and cassava farms and workday streets. I felt ashamed that my biological mother's family owed some of their wealth to this trade, in the Caribbean primarily.

As we passed, the sellers pulled my arm: *Madame! Smell dey—it no be proper-proper American? It be Levi's!*

We would ask in vain for indigo among the cloth sellers. "I'm looking for indigo—Nigerian cloth. Tie and dye," Eurama would say.

"Ah! I go show you." And the woman would return with any kind of batik or hand-stitched or -stenciled cloth. Never blue.

"Yes, but indigo! Is this not yellow?" Eurama would say.

They would return with green.

"No, indigo. Not 'leaf'!" Eurama would say.

They would find us gray.

"But this is 'ash'. Find blue!"

They would find us pale violet.

"My dear, find 'sky'!"

They would bring us cool, dark synthetic blue, spun on a Chinese factory machine.

It is true that each culture perceives color differently, and that the spectrum of color is divided arbitrarily. Color can be a *space*, and that space, however wide, however narrow, can hold one name or many. It all depends on the world you're in.

"My dear," Eurama said, "this is *exactly* the color, but she wants the one the Nigerian people make. The tie and dye."

"Ah, that cloth is *colo! Kitikwa!* You know, out of fashion. We Ghanaians left it with the colonial masters. So unless you get in some old lady's porto-manto. Yes, you French people say *portmanteau*, isn't it? Her old suitcases-o!"

In the months before I met Eurama, I had had days filled like this. Circles of misunderstanding. But now, for the first time, I knew that it was not a dance of wills but a problem of languages, of senses.

A woman who had been listening to us piped in, "Sister, there is a madame—her name is Salimata. A Nigerian. She sells those imported laces and ceremonial cloths. She will have proper indigo."

Eurama and I set off for Insurance, a vast cement building in the market, nearly a city block wide, that she'd directed us to.

"Ah! Salimata. I go show you," a man assured us, then led us down a passageway with signs of cloth sellers at its end.

But the Salimata he knew turned out to be one of three sisters who owned a currency exchange bureau that doubled as a wig shop.

"I think you want this other Salimata who used to sell here," she advised. "The Accra Metropolitan Authority sacked the cloth traders a few months ago. Unless you go to Thirty-first December Women's Market. The women left here are all from Togo, and they are only selling *materials*. If you want *cloth*, go there."

I looked at the bolts of imported calicoes and polyester blends beloved by Ghanaians. They would have them sewn into styles featured in the Macy's and Butterfield's catalogs that were collected from Western plants and sold like *obruni wawu* to West African shopkeepers desperate for paper to wrap food and wares.

I looked at Eurama and shook my head, stuck on this funny absolute: materials versus cloth.

This was not at all my world.

In those months Eurama was teaching me how to *look*, peeling back Ghana's layers with each interaction. Every day my eyes were doing a literal sharpening, like the slow adjustment to a new pair of glasses. As your senses dilate, it is as if you are given a new way of feeling, of being. It was part of what seeing in blue was, I imagined.

But not even new eyes revealed anything of indigo. It was as if the color—not just dark blues but true indigo, with all its depth, like the complex cut of the diamond— had been wholly wiped off the palate. I was in the world of that woman of legend, hungering in my simple white cotton cloth for a sky that was tantalizingly out of reach.

Eurama sat down on a bench. She sighed and wiped my face with her handkerchief. "The cloth you are talking about, it is not just sold *anywhere*. Local cloth—Ghana tie and dye and the rest, you can get it. But these proper old styles-o—they are never just in the market! You wait. After Ramadan I will find you the Hausa traders, and those old, old Soninke men who carry them down from Mali and from Guinea."

I spent hours sitting beside the sewing table in Eurama's shop watching her sister, Lady Diana, sew. Senam, the tailor across the street, sewed "styles": jeans with African prints on the pockets, shirts with expensive bead embellishments, the latest Fendi dress designs in batik patchwork. He specialized in couture and American and European ready-to-wear sewn to Accra tastes. Lady

Diana sewed *kaba* and slit, a coastal dress that had become Ghana's predominant national dress. It had a tight, structured bodice, waspishly setting off the waist, that exploded with flourishes at the sleeves and neck and sometimes the hips. It shaped the buttocks, and the skirt tapered to the ankles. A long slit up the back or at the sides revealed flashes of ankle and calf. It had probably originated in the seventeenth century; its Victorian roots were imprinted in the often rigid, straitjacket form of the body of the *kaba*, but it was Ghanaian to its core. However much Christian-missionary modesty had transformed Ghana's national dress in the colonial era, and no matter how much modern Christian and Muslim women might observe their own laws of decorum and cover (a glimpse of a thigh was shameful, and tank tops and jeans were the domain of prostitutes, despite their abundance in the *obruni wawu* markets), there was nothing as suggestive, or as un-Victorian, as the wide necklines and hoisted breasts and bold patterning moving tautly over powerful hips and thighs.

Even the most modern Ghanaian woman takes off her suit or slacks or minidress and returns to *kaba* and slit, the formal clothing of the office, church meetings, customary rites for births and deaths, weddings, anniversaries, and any moment of formal gathering. And so with luck one of the "Heavy Madames," the rich women who favored styles that proved their cosmopolitanism and who flocked to Senam's shop, would later cross the gutter to order a *kaba* from Lady Diana. The area women provided a constant parade of orders and fittings, and the vendors who frequented the shop with new button and zipper styles, threads, and other notions kept me beside Lady Diana for hours. She did vigorous business from Monday until Thursday, altering sleeves, widening necklines, adding lace and embroidery, changing trimming—whatever was in demand for the usual three-day-weekend-long marathon of funerals and memorial services, baby-naming ceremonies, church programs, engagements, and weddings.

Once when I was on the cusp of my teens, on a family trip to Scotland in the 1990s, I'd sat with my parents in a pub near a table shared by two African couples. I felt excited and anxious about being so close to Black people—to Africans, real continental Africans, no less, and self-conscious of my new Afro and my Waspy family. They were people from a world I knew I was a part of. I had carried in me the confusion of the many things I was named—Afro-American, Black, colored, mulatto—but understood that they were names for African people. Africa did not at all enter the landscape of Attleboro, the provincial and nearly all-white town in which I grew up in Massachusetts, except for an occasional body behind the windshield of a car passing through. Now I was deliciously near. The men wore a trilogy of patterned wool down to the tops of their platform shoes. One woman wore an awesome reddish curled wig, the other a green-and-red-plaid wool scarf wrapped in a high beautiful arch over her head. The women's headpieces framed smooth, dark faces, penciled with heavy black brows drawn nearly to their temples. I admired the waxy-sheened, bright dresses they wore, which revealed sweaters at their wide embroidered and laced necklines. It was an odd way to wear a sweater, on the inside, I thought. But their dresses were so beautiful and the logic of it made simple, new sense to me, reweaving the dull, familiar textures of home, where our closets were full of sweaters from the British Isles, Scottish tweeds and herringbone, L.L.Bean, Burberry coats—the darks and plaids of my adoptive parents' upper-middle-class world and their parents' origins.

I had worn these things uncomfortably, a kid in search of my own expression. I watched these women and noticed then the way that cloth became a skin, not just a covering or an accessory. For them, plaid was not an identity or a symbol to put distance on, the way it was for me. I wanted to feel free in my skin and in clothing the same way. It was patterning. Color. Simple adornment to make one's own.

At home I tried to mimic the women's styling, going to my mother's closet to retrieve a kilt she had once worn, adding a scarf of another color, a bright orange sweater, my red snakeskin shoes. Soon afterward I wore the outfit on a visit to my grandmother. In her most withering tone, she said, "Is that what they're wearing these days?" It was a standard line for her. When I tried to defend my style, she pulled a face of disgust. "You are part Black, I know, but do you think you are at all an African?"

I thought about my grandmother now and how she had helped set me on this road to indigo. Born at the turn of the century on an Arizona cattle ranch to British émigrés, she led many lives. Later, arriving in Brooklyn, New York, she traded schoolteaching and commuting by horse for Connecticut housewifery. She turned New York City elevator company owner when she was widowed in her late forties. She was quite a fancy clotheshorse and quite conscious of the quality of everyone's "threads," adorning her own with turquoise studs and Navajo jewelry.

Just before I left for Ghana, I had visited her, using the excuse of helping her to do some housework as a way to spend extra time and quell my anxiety that, already well into her nineties, she might be an ocean away from me when she died. She related to me through questions, asking over and over for mundane details of my life, responding with reserve until something moved her to speak. That day, as we were sorting through things stored in my mother's childhood bedroom—work I enjoyed because it elicited a rare quasi-intimacy—she started in on my Fulbright research. She seemed not to understand it, but I suspected it was a way to comment on my decision to do this work in Africa.

Among my mother's things, left in her childhood bedroom that had been preserved since she left home to work and then marry, were Fair Isle sweaters, plaids from her college sojourn in Scotland, more of my grandmother's southwestern inheritance, and a pair of Levi's jeans from the 1950s, carefully preserved. I pulled them from the drawer.

"Grandma, look at these! Look at what I am wearing.

These are Japanese jeans, they are dyed with pure indigo, and I won't tell you how much they cost, but I bought them at Bendel's, which is a store I know you approve of. You can smell the indigo dye!"

She curled up her nose. "I know what that smell is. I'm a ranch girl, you know."

"Well, everyone seems to want to recapture that pure thing of the past. People are clamoring for these kinds of jeans. There is a company that sells them for nearly six hundred dollars. Do you know what someone would pay for these old Levi's?"

"Are you going to sell them to get money for Africans?"

I laughed quietly to myself. My grandmother was hopeless. But I remembered when I had traveled to Ghana for the first time in the early 1990s, my old worn Levi's had been worth more than what I might pay in cash for anything. Everywhere I went I'd received offers for them. They were singular emblems of American cool.

"Grandma! What I'm saying is that I want to understand where our blue passion comes from."

"Well, it's not from Africa. I can send you to the ranch instead. We wore jeans to protect our legs when we were riding. You've never tried to know those people."

"Grandma, all over the world, jeans are king, and they all descend from indigo. Christopher Columbus's *Santa Maria* was rigged with denim sails when it arrived at these shores. Levi Strauss built a fortune on the stuff. Look at him! He was your father's contemporary—a Bavarian from a New York City dry goods family who went west in search of freedom and fortune. He arrived in San Francisco with one bolt of denim and sold most of it as tent material to raise funds for a stake in the gold rush. He sold a piece and sewed pants for a miner in 1873. Got a patent for his riveted pants with his partner Jacob Davis. The rest was history."

"Yes, that is America."

"Well, that is a piece of history that Africa is a big part of."

"Well, you do know how to live life, a-brown. Are you taking those jeans with you?"

"A-brown?"

"A-brown. It's an old expression, it means someone is living a high life."

"Let's say a-blue, Grandma!"

"Yes, you spent too much on those jeans, and you need to stay away from Bendel's. Anyway, I'm very proud of your Fulbright, even if it's taking you to Africa. You can bring your mother's jeans if you like."

The jeans stayed among my mother's things, but what I carried with me was the sense of my family's inheritance. Just as my grandmother would disavow my jeans, with her own closet full of Bendel's, our family would think of the history of indigo, of our own relationship with fashion and clothing and material culture, as an almost vulgar enterprise. I decided I was going to embrace beauty and history all at once.

Lady Diana's dress charts arrived every few weeks in the hands of vendors, who carried them to the streets like breaking news. I would excitedly study them.

The basic form of *kaba* and slit never changed, but the sleeves and necklines and tucks and hems were refashioned with intricate hand-smocking and aproning and pleating, new button and ribbon imports. The styles were named and renamed: Cash Madame, Sweetheart, Ready to Eat, Three Sisters (with three rows of heavy ruffles at the skirt). Women clamored to stay with the trends.

I was shy of dressing in African clothing, which would invite *obruni* jokes ("Can you walk in *kaba* and slit? The slit is tight-o, and you don't have a big bottom to balance you!") that Eurama insisted were admiration. But *kaba* and slit was intoxicating. I didn't like all the styles—many of the newer fashions were too fussy, and the layers of cloth that women wore and the lining needed to stiffen the bodice and skirt and add volume to the shoulders and hips and behind seemed uncomfortably hot. What I liked most was the way African women's dresses, their coverings, or wrappers, or head ties, were constantly being retied, repositioned, refashioned as they were worn, with movements as reflexive as repocketing a handkerchief or pulling up a sleeve. I wanted to learn that vernacular of dressing, which was so kinetic and personal and felt similar to listening to a story being told, where the teller reinvents and embellishes and plays on your ears as they deliver it to you.

The rites of sewing and dressing, my idleness at Eurama's, and my frustration with the pace of my work left me wanting to pierce wider the veil of this cult of cloth. One day I gave Lady Diana a piece of synthetic indigo print that I'd found in Makola market and picked a style from the chart.

"Lady Diana, please make me *kaba* and slit."

She took the cloth, smiling at me only very slightly, and put it in a basket under her sewing table. I knew that something was yet to be said.

When I returned at lunch, Eurama waved the cloth in her hand. "Hey, my friend, we cannot sew this. No."

"What's wrong?" I asked.

"This be *nyama-nyama* cloth! It be shit."

"I know it is just a cheap tie and dye, but the pattern is very nice," I said.

"We only sew *kaba* from good things," she said with finality. "We don't use local cloth."

She dug furiously into Lady Diana's sewing bag. "My dear, if you want *kaba*, this cloth will be sweet on you." She pulled out a floral print, a factory reproduction of a batik, with wild reds and deep blues. "This cloth is called 'Koforidua flowers.'"

She saw I was unmoved.

"Oh! You mean you don't like this? 'Koforidua flowers'—hei! Koforidua girls are very, very lovely! They wear heavy, heavy gold because of all the cocoa money there—and diamond money too. They are very black, and the gold looks good against their skin. This is why this cloth was given this name. It's fine-o! And the colors suit you."

I was not enthusiastic.

"*Esowara*," Eurama laughed and muttered. "It's up to you! Anyway, I will take you to find something. Christabel has begun to menstruate. I want to buy cloth for her; she can wear *kaba* now to church. My Lady Diana too will marry soon enough. Her boyfriend has asked me for the list of things that his family must bring as dowry."

"Maa, I don't like *kaba-o!*" Christabel protested. She was a lovely girl, with a delicate head and eyes like huge pools of dark sap, her body long and lithe. She was wearing a denim dress that she'd saved for by selling homemade toffees at the shop, convincing Senam to sew it for her from his scraps.

"When your hips come, you will like *kaba*! And even if you don't wear it, you have to at least begin your cloth box. When you have a cloth box, it shows you are mature. Every respectable woman has cloth. Plenty of cloth! For Ghana women, it is the most important thing after having children. Cloth is more than our bank account and our insurance. Even if you don't own land, you own cloth. You could say it is like a European lady's silverware! The price of fine cloth never decreases, while our money, its value keeps on changing. If you have three hundred pieces of good cloth, like a real madame, well then you have something!"

It made me think of my biological father, an artist and one of the early Black interior decorators who, even into his eighties, still prides himself on dressing "editorial" every day, in suits and fancy hats, bedecked in diamonds and turquoise jewelry, a nod to his Choctaw mother. As with many West African women, most of my father's wealth hangs in his closet.

"And when you die-o! Cloth will go to your grave

with you—we take our finest to the afterlife. But cloth itself never dies. Your children inherit it and keep you near to them. When you die, they will open your cloth box and see how you have lived! Every wedding, every birth, those who die, church occasions, new presidents, festivals, anniversaries, customary rites—each one has its cloth, and your cloth will tell your story. My old lady— the aunt who raised me—when she dies, you will see she has hundreds of cloths! She has married—twice! She has eight children. She is a mother-o! She has cloth from my mother and grandmother. More than a hundred years of family life! Her cloth will show you how she is respected. So my dear, don't argue when I tell you I'm going to sew *kaba* for you!"

Later, we three visited the cloth stores in Makola. "This is proper-proper Holland," she said, pointing to cloths that could only be called African, lining a glass case.

"Holland."

"Holland, my lady!" she exclaimed, pointing to the finished edge of the cloth. "100% Guaranteed Real Dutch Wax. Vlisco. That is the finest! Then GTP—Ghana Textiles Printing. This is Vlisco too, but it's made here in Ghana, at Tema Harbor. GTP is second. Then we have what we call 'small Holland.' These are the copies that the Nigerians and Chinese and Indians make. And then there are all these cheap-cheap things." She waved dismissively at the lighter-weight cloths, their colors not as brilliant, thin enough to require heavy polyester linings when they were sewn.

She selected a pale yellow and brown and red version of the spider design I'd been seeing from the stack of GTP.

"This is an old design," Eurama said. "My grandmother wore this. Her grandmother wore it. When people see it, they will admire it; it is a cloth every woman will collect. She can wear it to church. The spider is Ananse, the trickster, who is part of our folklore. I'll buy this for Christabel."

As Eurama counted her bills to pay for the cloth I calculated it cost her more than a week of profits from the shop.

"As for you, you are from New York, so you are already a madame! And you like fine things like indigo. Well, indigo is finished at the moment, so your spirit demands Holland!" She pointed to the edges of cloths in a brilliant colored stack, the fold of each six- and twelve-yard piece hard and hefty like the spine of a book, and called out their names.

"'Capable husband.'"

"'Sorry, I'm taken.'"

"'Free as a bird.' Sika tu se anumaa. Or, 'Money flies like a bird.'"

"'Your foot, my foot.' Or, 'When my husband goes out, I go out.'"

"Ahwene pa nkasa. 'Fine beads don't make noise.' That means 'A true lady knows how to carry herself with reserve.' Try to follow this advice." She punched my arm playfully.

"'Men are not like ears of corn.' You see-o! You can pull

back the husk, but you don't get to see the rotten insides until you've already brought it home." The kernels in the design looked like teeth in an abstract grinning mouth.

"Okuunu paa. 'Good husband.' Some women will wear this to show appreciation, or to make their husband feel like a big man. Or they buy it and pretend their husband is buying them cloth, but maybe he is really spending his money on girlfriends, or her co-wife is abusing her, so she bought it to upset her."

" 'Death steps.' Or 'Stairs to heaven.' Everyone has to travel them."

"Oba paa. 'Good woman.' This one was from the sixties. We named it for Queen Elizabeth's visit."

" 'Nothing in my hand I bring.' This is an old cloth, from before my grandmother's day. During independence we used to say, 'It takes the whole hand and not single fingers to build a nation,' but now we're in poverty and it has a whole new meaning."

"ABC. Suukuu nko na nyansa nko. 'Attending school does not mean one will be wise.'"

"Sraada. This is 'Carpenter's saw.' Like life, it goes up and down."

"Okla ete ablotse. 'My spirit has traveled abroad even if my body has not.'"

"Afa me nwa, 'You have taken me as cheap and easy as the snail.'"

"Hand and egg. 'Hold life like an egg—your destiny is in your hands.'"

"I like this one," I said, admiring a bright purple and yellow cloth with tiny geometric designs.

"Dwene wo ho. No, it is not good for you!" Eurama said.

"Why?"

"This cloth says, 'Think about yourself.' People will look at you and laugh.

'Awo, the *obruni* says, 'Think about yourself'! This one will be better. It is an old-old design from the fifties. 'Nkrumah's pencil.' That is the cloth we wore after independence—the design is like the pen our first Black president used to sign the British away. The pen is mightier than the sword! But later, when Nkrumah was getting mad and putting everyone in prison, it became his pen to sign away freedom."

"Eurama, you are a historian!"

"As for me, I left school when I was eleven years old. My mother had died, and my father had another family. My aunt who adopted me—I call her my mother—well, she sent me to work to pay my brother's school fees. But I know cloth, Papa!"

Indigo cloths, like the professor's, also had names and meanings: 'No more velvet,' a finely detailed cloth that sprang out of a Nigerian sumptory imports ban. 'Ibadan city is sweet,' celebrating a legendary Yoruba town. 'Holding up the sun,' a celebration of the strands of tiny beads that women wear seductively at the waist, that a lover can roll and play with and count. 'Praise the goddess Olukun,' the Yoruba deity who is owner of the oceans, the mediator of life and death, the goddess of patience and wisdom, who oversees dreams and fertility. The cloths spoke of commercial longings, and history, the spiritual, and domestic conflicts. What I thought had been lost with the disappearance of indigo—the *language* of the cloth, the very African-ness of its vernacular—was in fact still alive in these Dutch wax cloths.

"Ah, this one is named for a beautiful hotel in Freetown, in Sierra Leone, where people used to go and dance high-life and enjoy after independence. 'City Hotel'! We have one too, in Ghana."

In the spiraling, almost whimsical weblike yellow floral pattern on a hot pink background was an ode to the promises of independence and modernity and its aspirations. I thought of Graham Greene's novel *The Heart of the Matter*, set in this very hotel. He had lived at City Hotel in the 1940s during the last three years of World War II as a colonial officer and suspected secret agent. It was the place where he'd written *The Ministry of Fear*. The hotel became a landmark and it would burn down later that year in my first year in Ghana in a fire caused by squatters who were refugees from the long civil war.

I decided "City Hotel" was the cloth I would buy. It was a beautiful countertext to Greene's stories. I had known Africa first and primarily by novels—African and Western ones—and now I was learning the stories and histories embedded in a different kind of text. Cloth could tell a story and make social meaning. In some cases, they were literal monuments to social history. The stories had a depth I had not realized—they were complex, cloaked in a superficial beauty, so that they were inscrutable to the illiterate. I wanted to read them, and to be read wearing them, to make their stories my own.

Eurama asked the owner for twelve yards.

"We can each take six yards and sew *kaba*," she said. "It's called making an anchor. You sew the same cloth with your friends or your family or church or whoever to show your closeness to them."

The cloth cost more than the rent on my small apartment in Accra, more than a third of a median Ghanaian annual income.

Eurama was standing looking at me with seriousness after I paid. "My dear, you have eyes, but you don't see! Look at this blue!"

I looked at the cloth again. Indeed, there was a fine, crackling, gently bleeding blue line that laid the foundation of the batik and became a wonderful filigree-like setting for the explosion of other colors. Vlisco would become my modern lead back to indigo.

That afternoon, as we sat, exhausted from the market, on the bench in front of Eurama's, a woman passed wearing an old Yoruba cloth like one from my professor's house.

"Please, stop the person for me!" I begged.

Eurama looked at me with pity. "You this girl, they will think you are a mad person! In Ghana here, we believe a person's spirit is in their cloth. And true, if you say you admire something, the person will feel obliged to give it to you. Especially if you are *obruni*. This is how we are. How can you ask a person for their cloth? And you—do you have something to give her when she nakeds herself for you?"

But even as she was protesting, she called to the woman. "Oh, Catherine, you want to disgrace me! Shame on you!" she hissed.

When the woman approached us, Eurama acted sheepish. "Mi paachoe! I beg you, excuse her, eh? She is *obruni*, and she is a student—studying our local cloth. Eh, heh. She is admiring your dress."

The woman laughed at the strangeness of the encounter. "Ah, it is an old-old cloth. It was my mother's cloth. And you see I am not at all young!"

"Thank you sooo much. Madame! Thank you. You have helped her," Eurama said smiling. I could tell she was heading me off, afraid I would ignore her warning.

I was ready for her editorializing.

"My dear Catherine, what you don't understand is that this cloth—maybe her mother got it when she gave birth to her, and it was passed on when she died. The cloth is having some spirit in it. It belongs to an ancestor. You see-o! It is not a small thing. Can she give you her own mother's spirit, even her body?"

My face burned with shame.

"Blue! Blue! Maybe we will have to find you a blue husband. Like you'll marry a Niger man. Would you like it? They wear proper-proper indigo. They wear it until it paints them. The man will romance you, and your whole body will be blue-o!"

"If you wait until the Harmattan, we will find you a Niger man—hey!" Lady Diana laughed from her sewing table. "The Harmattan is 'the doctor,' it blows cool wind from the Sahara, and it carries us many wonders."

"Don't mind her!" Eurama laughed. "It's only a lot of dust! It's just that it will be close to the holidays, and those Niger people always come selling their cows and their things."

# TWO

# A Burning Heart, Ghana

Just before Christmas, as the fasting for Ramadan ended, the world of the Blue Men, the Tuareg people, started to appear. First two boys at the gate of Barclays Bank, wearing matching dirty white tunics, bare feet in splayed-open sneakers cast in blue rubber, with blond-streaked afros and narrow faces that blended the African and the Semitic much like my own. The tiniest one hurled his bony frame at me and clung desperately to my waist, his legs seizing my thighs.

"Ma!" he wailed. His lips were pursed in a small O, his hand swept his mouth like a newborn's signing of hunger. The older boy stood a few paces away, pleading with his eyes.

"Please," he said in a choking whisper.

"*Obruni*, your children want to eat," a woman said, handing the older boy a coin. The boys exploded in grins.

Then a woman stood on the dangerous meridian at Kwame Nkrumah Circle, nursing a child, taking money from slowing cars. Her milk-white skin, her long, fine hair plaited in two and anchored by tiny brass ornaments that hung in front of her ears like a Hasidic man's earlocks. The dark vegetal blue of her dress made me feel a kind of anxious excitement, recalling Eurama's early promise of the traders from the north, as if my desires were advancing with the desert storm.

Every day I encountered another child or woman begging. Then two Tuareg men in one week arrived at Euramas shop, offering the same reading after greeting me: "You have a clean heart, your third eye too is clear, but you have three enemies—one of them be woman. Maybe your husband has taken a second wife or girl-friend? You have a problem with the womb." The men had looked at me, one with quiet amusement, the other weariness, as they waited for an exchange: a Coke, a boiled egg and bread, or some coins. Later, I met a woman with the same sharp features, the same earlocklike braids in a guard booth at the U.S. embassy compound. A vendor sold exquisite hand-tooled leather picture frames in front of the Libyan supermarket; a man in a fine-tailored bush coat began to pass my house in the morning in a slow-crawling Hummer with diplomatic plates; a lone man walked Sunyani Highway; another herded holiday goats to the market at Pig Farm.

They were mysterious in the way their name "Blue Men" suggests—especially the men, whose virile femi-ninity was much like the delicate gauze of their tagle-musts, the desert turbans they wound into spectacu-lar hives from five-meter lengths of gauzy cotton. The swaths crossed the face, covering all but the eyes, a band dropping open to reveal the mouth. They appeared unanchored from the world they passed through. Strangers too in the village of urban Accra. In fact, the particular mix of Islam and Sufism, the African and the

Arab-Semitic, marked their place at the frontier of the Sahara, wedged between uneasy alliances of north and south, Christian and Muslim, Arab and African. They were agents and conduits in the impassable hinterlands of the desert, drivers of the legendary ancient caravans that had carried indigo and other sumptuary items like gold and ostrich feathers and ivory to the Mediterranean, bound for European luxury markets beginning in the last century A.D. Their darker history places them as middlemen and raiders in the centuries-long Arab slave incursions from Africa's north and east.

But in Accra the Blue Men were not blue in any way. There was not a trace of the legendary blue leached from their clothes into their faces and bodies and hands. Instead, they wore simple, light-colored robes of factory-spun cotton and damask, indistinguishable from many Accra citizens. They had arrived from the increasingly inhospitable North, wracked by civil strife, locust blight, and desertification. The poorest of them had walked from their homes in Mali and Niger—hundreds of miles, some surely a thousand or more—across several nations, down to the coast.

Nearly everyone despised the Blue Men: "Ach, these people! We don't like them. So many of them white like that, but they are not civilized! They come here in December begging, looking for Christmas money, but they are not Christians. Then too, they are not Muslims. Well, some are Muslims, but no be proper-proper ones."

"They are *bush people*. See how they come to beg, wearing no shoes, their women walking bare-breasted!

Even my own grandmother in the village puts on cloth and slippers."

"These people are witchcraft-o! Take care."

They lasted in Accra for a short season—during Christmas and Ramadan, when benevolence and trade were at their greatest flows—then Ghana's government routinely ran them out.

One day Eurama wanted to help a friend with preparations for a wedding, so I offered to go to Makola to buy rice for her shop. "Can you do it?" Eurama said. "They will cheat you because you're *obruni*. Anyway, you can try, but I beg, don't spoil my money-o!"

I felt a tingling pride as I made my way easily to Insurance and priced bags of rice, haggling until I paid no more than Eurama would. I let a *kayayo* girl take the lead through the crush of Friday shoppers as we worked our way back to the taxis at the edge of Rawlings Park. At one moment I looked into the crowd, and there in the sea of vying, brightly tied heads moving toward us, I saw one that stood high above the others, wrapped with mounting precision until it resembled the funnel of a small cyclone. It was luminescent, with a purplish-metallic shine over inky dark cloth, flashing like a fish's scales in the sunshine.

I felt a kind of burning in my heart. I was looking at the King of Cloths, the prestige cloth of the Blue Men. It had been traded for centuries from Kano, a legendary center for indigo dyeing in northern Nigeria that had first been established in the fifteenth century by the concubines of a Hausa emir. It was built into an enduring dynasty and is now the last active, large-scale dyeing center in West Africa. Kano indigo was the most prized for *taglemusts*: the narrow, five-meter-long gauze-thin strips of hand-spun cotton—each strip a measure of prestige—were joined together up to a yard across then dyed the deepest blue. It was then beaten on a wooden board with indigo powder mixed with goat fat, giving the cloth a flinty shine like fresh pencil lead.

As the man came closer, I saw a deep blue-stained brown face, covered with wide, gold-rimmed dark glasses. The blue bled onto a sky-blue damask robe. He stood more than six feet tall, and the folds of his clothes added to his enormousness. The man's face was impassive; he did not look left or right but moved through the crowd with quiet force.

I walked as fast as I could behind him, trying to keep him in my eye amid the traffic of head loads. But I lost him within a hundred yards, interrupted by a truck pushing into the crowd to make a store delivery.

At Rawlings Park I paid the girl and crossed the street to stand in the shade beside the *suya* sellers who had gathered along a fence, roasting spicy meat kebabs, hoping the man might return.

I found a spot against a low wall and settled into watching. A group of *kayayo* girls played *ampe*, a child's game of jumping and hand-clapping. A boy rested nearby, twirling a stick with light, papery yellow flowers attached to it, sending them floating. A dream reader called out to the crowd. I got lost in the moment of surreal pleasures, until I felt a man standing a breath away from me.

I kept my eyes averted, not wanting to encourage an interaction. From the corner of my eye I saw knock-off Adidas rubber surf shoes too close to my own feet, the spindly calves below the hem of a parchment brown silk robe. The robe was worn, but with very fine hand embroidery along its edges. A goatskin bag hung at his waist, with the animal's legs and tail intact—ubiquitous fashion in the northern villages.

I realized that he was only seeking shade as he waited for his *suya* to roast. I met him with a full gaze and saw a gentle face, with thin lines at the corners of his eyes, and then, as I raised my eyes, the dark indigo *taglemust*. He bowed slightly and raised his clasped hands to his forehead—a greeting of deference, signaling peace.

I felt almost giddy, greeting him in my broken French. We struggled through a few sentences of the customary greetings, and then he sat down a small distance away, and we kept company in a kind of anticipatory silence.

Finally I spoke, motioning to his head. "I am looking for this kind of cloth. Do you know where I can find it?"

We struggled with the question over and over again, until he took a pen and wrote "350,000" on the greasy newspaper that held his *suya*. Three hundred fifty thousand Ghana *cedis*. This was more than a junior professional's monthly salary. Good cloth could easily cost this much: kente and fine laces and other prestige cloths could cost hundreds of dollars. Indigo *taglemusts* too were prestige items.

"I would like to buy some," I said.

He reached up to the small storm on his head and started to unwind the cloth. My heart burned with surprise and desire. People were now watching us. Two conspicuous strangers; the man baring his head in public; it just wasn't done. The women selling dish towels and cheap cutlery on mats nearby suddenly started talking excitedly. I could sense traffic slowing around us.

A woman called out to me, "*Obruni*, why? Do you need something from this man?"

"Sister," someone called, "be careful of these people. If you mix up with him, or allow him anything, he will catch your spirit. You will wake up in the night and walk-o! You will walk to Niger if you have to because you have made yourself *amariya*—someone's wife! Can you walk to Niger? You are *obruni*. Even me, an African, I cannot walk to Niger, Papa!" she said, entertaining the crowd. There was laughter and more jokes. I could sense the jokes turning to insults.

"Money will fool your hand!"

"This man is a witchcraft! Take care-o!"

But I was possessed already. Unwrapped, the man's *taglemust* was old and worn, soaked with his sweat, yet I felt such a desperate, mercenary desire for this one dirty, brilliant cloth.

The women's attention felt like rising heat. We were both losing our respect, and I wanted to walk out of the scene, but I felt obligated now, oddly protective of the man, and bound by my hunger. He and I rose and started to walk to a quieter corner of the park, but it only drew more attention as some of the people followed and others joined. I hurried to count out 350,000 *cedis*—several bundles of 5,000-*cedi* notes that bulged wider than my hands—under the shelter of my handbag. Small girls hawking plastic bags gathered around us, pressing for a sale. The man dropped a coin in one of the girls' hands.

"*Obruni sikaaatchey! Obruni* millionaire!" someone from the crowd laughed, as he wound the *taglemust* into a ball and put it in the bag.

"*Donnez chapeau,*" the man said, smiling, patting his goatskin. He loaded the *cedis* inside it and took out a bright orange baseball cap embroidered with the logo of a hotel in St. Bart's, bowed, and kissed my hand. Then he turned and walked across the park and back toward the flow of the market, appearing tiny, suddenly almost frail, as he moved away.

I could still hear people's jokes and excited laughs. My face burned with shame and a strange excitement. I had one of the Kings of Cloth.

When I arrived home, Eurama was waiting for me at the compound gate. "*Dondo!* Happy marriage!" she cried as I stepped from the taxi.

"Look at your face! You are smiling! So now, when we cannot find you, we will know your juju has sent you to follow this Niger man.

"You this girl—you are *strong!* This your juju— hmmmm! Aunty Ama, the egg seller, said she saw you in Makola. Shame! I hope it was not my rice money you spent."

I showed her the sack in the trunk of the taxi. She went to the wall at the side of the house and called to her son in the neighboring yard. "Kwesi-o, come! Carry this rice to the shop and then get a bucket and bring Catherine seawater!"

"Why do I need seawater?" I protested.

"Hummm," Eurama said. "We have to remove this man's spirit from the cloth—so the spirit doesn't turn you madder than you are. We will wash it three times and pray over it. Tomorrow morning I will call my pastor to also pray.

"Blue! Blue! Is there nothing else in life that matters? Or what? You are a witch? I just don't understand. You want every beautiful thing! And you want the ugly ones too." She turned her nose to the cloth. "Not your juju alone that needs devotion! If you are going to spend your money, you could get a cat to feed, or a dog at least! I won't mention a human being. Then God's blessings would come because you're caring for His creation. But cloth? Is this the only thing you know?"

I followed Kwesi to the beach, Eurama's words echoing. I didn't want to argue with her, and I didn't understand her wild quarreling. It was usually full of a kind of humor. The ongoing refrain that I was chasing folly, and the mere vessels of life's beauty, was spoken even as she helped me. Today what I had done had really disturbed her and some balance in our understanding. I felt a kind of melancholy as I dropped the *taglemust* into the tide, watching the sea swell and open its folds to their five-yard length. The cloth was the shade of the sea at the line of the horizon.

Was it Eurama's misunderstanding of me that hurt? Or my own sense of having acted like a stranger, like someone who had become the collector and sold their stake at being a citizen?

Every visit to that beach filled me with pleasure and an old feeling of gravity. I grew up spending summers on Cape Cod, and it had been a place of intense joy, a kind of psychic emblem of my childhood. In my early teens I became fascinated with the idea that there was a straight pull in the tides that ran from there to Africa, a place that occupied a large part of my consciousness even then. Because my mother is a historian, and she taught history everywhere we went, I began to piece it all together: the nearby Cape Verdean community; the shore from Massachusetts to Connecticut; the clothing mills that were part of the landscape of my childhood, where I would later discover my Jewish family legacy of mill owners and "rag traders"; the community of the Moses Brown School and Brown University, which she and I both attended, founded on the wealth of the Providence Brown family, who were Quakers with shipping and cotton concerns. It all had something to do with the transatlantic slave trade, a history that was very present if unseen. I began to feel disconnected from Cape Cod and resentful of my darker figure in the frame of a Waspy Eden. But when I first encountered the tides of the Guinea Sea, the African Atlantic, I felt those currents between the two shores mixing in ways I could contain.

The beauty of the *taglemust* moving in the tide, knotting and unfurling, was mesmerizing. Indigo was a part of that Atlantic. If there was a spirit at work, or an act of devotion to be made, mine would be bound to history—my own and that of the people I was seeking.

I hadn't made this journey simply to be a collector, but I needed indigo in my eye. I wanted to make something of history's wild skein, starting from just its literal bluest threads.

I'd do what Eurama asked, and let the ocean cleanse the cloth and me, and let her prayers clear my path.

Later that night, in the quiet of my room, I took the *taglemust* and spread it in the moonlight to dry. The ocean's roar blended with the gentle rhythms of my landlord's family turning in. I went to sleep with the cloth, briny with seawater, waving above me, a shrine to my devotion.

The next morning the power was back on and stable after days of sporadic current. Everyone was in a better mood.

"I'm sorry about yesterday," Eurama said. "Forgive me, eh? You see, my pressure was up. My husband promised me money, and Christobel's school fees are overdue—I've had to borrow from a friend, and now she needs her money. We are in need of a lot of things in this house, and he seems to just use it up with the lotto and drink—buying this ticket and that, at the bar all day and all night, paying for drinks for friends. He is even buying drinks for the woman who owns that bar at the top of the road, and she is playing him like a fool, making him think he has a girlfriend! All the area people are laughing about it. Everyone thinks it is witchcraft. How else can you explain what has happened to a man who used to be a big manager, with servants and a big car and nice house, who could feed and educate his five children? You have been here for some months now. How many times have you seen this man? Always at the bar, only coming home to sleep like a goat. Would you even think I was married? Did you know my children had a father?"

For the first time I saw Eurama's cracks. She always seemed to be making order of the world for everyone around her. She ran her shop and cared for her children and the many neighbors who came for credit and advice or a meal with the ease of a stateswoman. I'd only seen her husband, Mr. Ghilchreist, when he passed drunken through the gate at the side of the shop. The few times we'd spoken, his words were so garbled I could only look at him, pretending to understand.

"I can help you if you need me to," I offered gently.

Eurama made a gentle click with her tongue. "I didn't want to bother you. And I don't want to borrow from you or anyone. But really, if you can help me, with even fifty dollars, I want to buy into Lever Brothers and sell soaps and cooking oil—they have the best. People buy them! I'll split the profits with you starting off and pay you back small-small. We will be partners for a while."

The shop was suddenly choked with bodies. The radio had been buzzing all week with talk of Baby Ocansey, an Accra businesswoman who had allegedly gone into cahoots with government agents and defrauded a local bank of millions. People stopped at Eurama's and at the electrician next to Senam, where they spilled out into the road watching a TV hooked up to a generator and set out for sale next to the gutter, happy for news of any kind.

"Ah, I should send you to this woman!" she said excitedly. "Mercy Ocansey! She is a very fine dyer. She and Baby will be from the same family. They are Adangbes —from Ada, a town where the Volta River and the Atlantic meet. Ocansey means 'House of Money,' so you know them already. They are strong—a strong family! Anyway, never mind!" she continued cheerfully. "You are also strong. With a very powerful juju. She doesn't make proper-proper indigo, but she will teach you a lot of things."

Eurama was back to her old self now, making order of the world. She called Kwesi and sent word to Aunty Mercy at her place at Kuku Hill on the far side of Osu: I was a "student" doing research on textiles, and I would like to visit her factory and get help with my schoolwork. In less than an hour, Aunty Mercy sent her houseboy to us with a message: *Madame says that if you want to learn, you should come and make yourself an apprentice. She knows Aunty Eurama is sending you, so you must be a brilliant and worthwhile girl. Aunty Eurama is dear to us; Aunty Mercy will take you like family.*

Eurama smiled. "How much money does she want?"

"You come and discuss it with her."

"This woman is serious-o!" Eurama said. "Aunty Mercy will eat you like an Accra rat! You see our rats—they slip into your room and blow sweetly on you, then chew, blow sweet, and chew, until they have removed all the skin on your feet! But she is one of the only dyers left in town who really knows cloth."

I wondered about the Ocanseys. Ada had been a place of great value to the transatlantic slave trade and other commerce, like textiles—especially indigos, which were used as a form of currency. Adangbe families had profited alongside European traders from their control of the mouth of the river and route into the interior. What might Mercy teach me?

When Eurama and I went to Aunty Mercy's place the next morning, she was just waking. We were called to a bedroom in the back of her large compound, in an old colonial house heavily shuttered and dark inside, so that it was cool but stuffy. The bare, hanging fluorescent bulbs glared against a turquoise wash on the walls and French-made Louis XIV furniture replicas upholstered with pink velvet, a style that was popular among the francophone African elite. Mercy sat on a couch fashioned from the seat of a minivan covered with a patchwork of her batiks.

Aunty Mercy looked eerily like Miles Davis—the same large, intent eyes; mouth taut like a bow; the deep, muddyish olive-brown-black skin pulled tight over elegant long bones; a wavy mane falling from an oddly high hairline. Even inside that dim room she wore vintage 1970s dark glasses with gold rims, wide windshields on a face ready to strike.

"Ah, so you've brought this your *obruni*! Welcome!" she said.

Eurama and I sat with Aunty Mercy for the whole of the morning, as the various house girls came and went, calling her for her bath, bringing a steamed fish breakfast, showing her samples of cloth newly sent from her factory, serving her beer, ushering the yam or tomato or bread seller to the door so she could survey what had been purchased for the house. The seamstresses, who worked in the courtyard behind Aunty Mercy's shop at the front of the compound, would appear in shifts with a newly sewn dress, needing her approval.

I tried not to betray my passion for the brilliant tie-dye and batik cloths being shown. Aunty Mercy's blues were not indigo, but they were brilliant. I saw a parade of her reds and oranges and browns: a peach-and-wine-colored cloth stamped with the Johnson Wax logo; another in orange and pink for Faytex sanitary napkins that had been commissioned for the local plant workers to wear.

I sat on her bed, watching, surprised by her informality, not at all typical of Ghanaian social exchanges. I loved the intimacy of the household and the way every transaction required so much *contact*. I peeked at the wigs and scarves and cosmetic bottles stuffed into the space between the wall and the mattress, hiding my voyeurism behind Aunty Mercy's stack of ancient style books. *Welcome Abroad* [sic]. *Masculine Dress Styles*. Lagos couture of the late 1980s featured short-haired women wearing longish tunics and wide-legged trousers, like a classic West African man's suit, called an *up and down*, complete with spats and a walking stick. The older Abidjan books showed women in full boubous, with sacrilegious bell-bottom trousers showing at the hem where delicate *pagnes*, traditional two-yard cloth wrappers, should have been.

"Ah, so you want to learn about indigo," Aunty Mercy finally said. "Indigo is for those who can afford. I only wear indigo and these my own cloths."

She had slipped on a boubou of oxblood-red-batiked damask with the long, ballooning sleeves popular with Senegalese women. She opened a wardrobe and took down two pieces of indigo that had been worn soft and textured like denim, patterned with subtle, lighter blue clouds. She began tying them, one full at her waist, the other across her head like a large, jaunty nurse's cap. Then she covered herself in a cloud of Joy perfume.

"I never used *lavender* until I met this Holland man. My husband-o! Every day for perfume! He would tell me, 'Try to use this. This is not Africa. You have to smell like a European flower.' Ah, a husband. You can't trade a husband for anything.

"This indigo, you won't get it anymore. This cloth is very old. Formerly we had indigo. Real-real indigo—you will only find it being done in the bush. In the northern parts. In Accra here, it's every day for Europe! We like what you people like. If you love something, we Ghanaians perfect the love. In Ghana here, indigo, brown, wine, green, black—these are colors for mourning mostly. But you people wear them plenty. I've come to appreciate them.

"I married my Holland man in the sixties and went to Holland with him. Me, I didn't have any education, so I went to work at the Vlisco factory. I saw how they do their cloth. The wax, the technique—it is taken from batik, only they have money for better dyes, better cotton, and it is done on those heavy machines. I said, 'Hei! I am an African. I know the kind of beauty that is our beauty.' So when my husband disappointed me, I came home and started my factory and fucked them all!"

"Madame, someone is here to buy!" a girl called from outside the door. We followed Aunty Mercy into the shop, where she reclined on a colorful woven floor mat and ordered the helpers and the seamstresses around as more customers began to arrive. She reached constantly between chair cushions and under edges of the carpet, where she'd tucked wads of *cedis* and foreign bills of every kind; then she'd call out orders for beer, more food, a special zipper so a Swedish woman's purchase could be made into a dress. By early afternoon I counted nearly six million *cedis* in sales—mostly to diplomatic corps wives and Ghana's elite, who appreciated Mercy's art and would pay her prices for the unusual colors that she achieved with her store of imported dyes. Six million *cedis* was more than the monthly fortune that Fulbright paid to me.

Aunty Mercy represented an older generation of Ghanaian women, those "heavy Madames" who were descended from, sometimes inheritors of family guilds. They had been able to gain significant footholds in the economy before the collapse of the guilds, the opening of immigration (their children chose to go abroad rather than inherit the business), the country's economic depression in the 1980s, and the effects of globalization. Eurama had told me that a certain huge mansion I'd wondered about—striking because it sat among crude cement and mud structures in Ada, just two hours east of Accra—was Aunty Mercy's "family house." Family property was typically as old as a family line unless ethnic conflict or colonialism had interrupted the ownership. I had done a bit of research on the Ocanseys. Aunty Mercy was the descendant of a family that had surely colluded with the transatlantic slave trade. Her Accra property— a former colonial residence—and her business would be a living part of that legacy. Even the house girls, who she said were "family" who had been "sent to her from the village"—an arrangement typical in Ghanaian house-holds—were likely to be descendants of once-inden-tured clan members. Under the modern arrangement they would work from puberty until marriage for little or no wages, in exchange for "training" and a parting contri-bution to the girl's start in business or her dowry.

Aunty Mercy's legacy was old and new.

She was my first glimpse of African bohemia. Her seamstresses would emerge with copies of dull, outdated Western dress styles, and she would rearrange a sleeve or collar, order them to restitch it, and turn out some fabu-lous innovation. She was the funky, splendid Miles Davis of cloth, where each stitch, like his every note, undid the expected sound.

I sensed that she suffered for her individuality.

And from drink, judging by her ten o'clock request for beer.

She asked me if I was ready to begin my apprenticeship, and I'd known even before I'd come there that I would not do it.

"I'm interested in learning about indigo. But you don't ever dye indigo here?" I asked.

"I can do it, but it be money matters! It is a long process, and nowadays if people get money to buy cloth, they are going to run to buy Holland."

I could witness batik dyeing most anywhere in Ghana, and I had taken textile-dyeing classes. Mercy seemed hardly to work herself anymore, just supervising what came from the factory. What I wanted from her—her stories, and her way with cloth—I could get sitting right there in her shop. I planned to return and try to dig into the family's history.

I told her that my student money could not support an apprenticeship, and she looked disappointed. She made a counteroffer, and when I refused, we all sat quietly, Eurama's eyes laughing.

From a radio in the courtyard, a song, "Just One More Dance," was playing.

It was a colonial relic, a duet famously covered by Harry Belafonte and Miriam Makeba. A woman, out dancing with her lover as her husband lay dying, is urged home again and again. For weeks, Joy FM, the local radio station, had been mixing the song with its usual playlist of "hiplife"—popular tunes that were a blend of rap and hip-hop and Ghana's famous horn-driven dance music called "highlife," which originated in the 1900s. They played a British version from the 1950s, and each time it broke over the airwaves the young would moan and old timers would break into old steps. They would sing along and begin to reminisce about the old dance halls and old lovers, Independence and later coups. Aunty Mercy danced a few slow winding steps, her body moving effortlessly, her hand handkerchief spinning gracefully in the air.

She lowered her beer glass and looked up to the sky. "Serious-o! A husband is not a small thing. For me, if I had a husband, I would not play around. If he died-o, I would mourn him properly."

"You see this woman? She has had four or five husbands already," Eurama quipped. "As for me, I have just one, and he married drink long ago."

Aunty Mercy didn't seem to hear her. She stood up and moved a heavy clay planter with her foot, revealing a small key. She went to unlock a wardrobe at the back of the shop and pulled out an exquisite woven cloth like one worn by the women I'd seen in Mali. In a field of bright royal blue were elliptical white markings, like the dance of a small bird's feet, tapping out a cosmic message or sign.

Eurama grabbed playfully at my breast. "Hei! My friend, see how your whole body is shaking! I tell you, someone has made cloth your lover."

Aunty Mercy laughed, "Ah, this be proper-proper indigo. It is fine-o! I might sell it to you, but it will be very expensive and you are only a schoolgirl, you say. Ah, you won't get it easily. You won't see it—no, you won't see indigo at all nowadays. Unless there is a funeral."

I felt like I was in the grip of the same fever from the day at Makola. Eurama was eyeing me. I calculated how much it might cost, how much I might pay, what I would trade—of my budget, of my dignity, of my pose as a schoolgirl—to have it.

"Ah, Gifty!" Mercy called. "Gifty, show *obruni* my blue beads. This girl likes blue! She's a student so maybe she can afford at least beads-o!"

"Please, her money is toooo small," Eurama insisted, "even for beads."

She had saved me from myself. She rose to leave, and Aunty Mercy took my hand.

"Come back, *obruni*. Come and visit anytime. I like you, eh? I will find you indigo. Fine-fine indigo."

# THREE

# Widow's Blues, Ghana

I was awakened before dawn at the sound of Eurama at my window, calling for me to unlock the gate. The sun was only half-risen, and she was dressed in a very formal *kaba* and slit. Her face was tight with worry.

"Mr. Ghilchreist is sick-o! Please, bathe and come quickly. I need you to come to the hospital!"

In the weeks since Eurama had confessed her troubles to me, Mr. Ghilchreist had started to appear more and more. He had become more slender and wizened, walking drunk, past Eurama's shop every afternoon, tipping his hat at us before he retired to his bedroom. Occasionally he appeared at the back door of the shop, sheepishly handing over money for a razor or soap.

"Did you see that spirit passing? It resembles my husband," Eurama would joke. "Now that I'm not bothering him for money, he feels free to roam. He knows you're helping me and yesterday he said to me, "Suppose Catherine had a prick? You would have a proper new husband. I like her and I wouldn't argue.'"

When I arrived at the house I found Mr. Gilchreist half-sitting in the backseat of his old Volvo sedan, wearing a handsome suit. He reminded me of older

African-American men at home who dressed formally for the bank or the doctor—an assertion of dignity and a wearing of armor that had been a legacy of American colonialism. He was ashen, and his hair seemed to have whitened overnight. His legs were shaking, and he tried to get control over them, finally grabbing his knees and lifting his feet in behind him. He sat childlike as we rode, Eurama's nephew driving, across the city to a special new "big man's" clinic.

"Don't you have a beautiful wife and five children, a good job? Shame on you!" the doctor said to Mr. Ghilchreist as Eurama and I were called into his office. The formality and distance between the two of them was startling to me, but it said as much about male and female spaces in Ghana as the fact that it was assumed I would join them because I was the attending *obruni*.

Three nights before, the power had been cut, and I had sat with Eurama, selling by candlelight, when two young men appeared in the darkness. I didn't understand what was happening until we were halfway down the road, where the mechanics at the *fitter shop* behind Togetherness Bar stood with Mr. Ghilchreist. They had been working under torchlight when they saw him walk out of the back of the bar to urinate and fall into a ditch. The ditch was an artery for the city's refuse, deeper than two men, and as wide as a lane of a city street. The alcohol had seemed to rubberize him; he barely had a wound. But for the next two days he sat at home, not moving from a living room chair.

"He isn't sick. He is totally ashamed!" Eurama quipped.

"Otherwise he'd be right back there at Togetherness Bar spending the water money."

The doctor watched us over the top of his glasses. "I don't see anything obvious here besides what drink is doing to him, but I want him to go to Korle-bu Hospital for more tests. Our ambulance driver has not yet reported for work—an ambulance would be best because traffic is so impossible. I hope you have a private car?"

He shook Eurama's hand. "Be patient, madame. God will help."

After packing them into the car, I had said good-bye, glad he'd escaped the worst. Then I'd gone to see if the rumors were true and the university library had indeed reopened from the strike. As soon as I returned to Eurama's, I knew that something was wrong. The metal shutter was pulled across her shop. When I entered the yard, things seemed to have been hurriedly packed up. The peanuts or palm kernels, the giant wooden mortar and pestle for pounding yam and plantain into *fufu*, which would ordinarily be spread out drying near the gate in the last powerful glare of sunshine, were not there. The clotheslines, which usually created a wonderful, perfumed cloth maze between the shop and the house, had been stripped of everything.

I saw Eurama's frame just above the veranda wall. She was a dark silhouette, in a dark sheath, her head tied simply with a black crepe scarf. Her gold earrings and necklace, always flashing against her skin, were removed.

There were three women beside her. They studied a large X-ray film against the sunlight.

I moved toward them, my heart racing, instinctively wrapping my arms across my chest to soothe the ache. Kwesi emerged from the side of the house holding an enamel pan. Everyone stood frozen as he walked to the clothesline and pinned first a man's white undershirt, then a pair of gray socks, and then the gray bush jacket and trousers that Mr. Ghilchreist had worn that morning.

They hung dripping from the line, a desultory waving flag.

While they sat in traffic on a stretch of less than five miles of road, Mr. Ghilchreist had died. Eurama sat in the front seat of the car, not understanding when Kwesi had asked for directions to the mortuary at the hospital gate.

Heavy drops of water fell from Mr. Ghilchreist's clothes onto the ground, marking our silence.

*Shango is the death that drips* to, to, to
*Like indigo dye dripping from a cloth*

I had encountered these lines of a Yoruba praise song, or *oriki*, in a collection of Yoruba poetry long before, and the reference to indigo intrigued me, but the words hung without context, without bearing. Hearing the cold certainty of it now, they suddenly had a terrible meaning. *To, to, to.* It was sound, not words—the bleeding of a freshly dyed cloth into the red laterite earth. The words were meant to summon the power of Shango, the thunder god, the meter of justice: his ineffability, his unending force, the terror he inspires.

Indigo has an exquisite symmetry with death. It covers everything; its dark, inexplicable power will reach into every fiber, catch every hair, grab the skin. Its print is sure and indelible. Its stain transcends everything.

*To, to, to.* The drops marked my steps. When I stood in front of Eurama, I looked plainly at her, but she did not meet my eyes.

Suddenly a tiny, birdlike woman pushed open the gate with the force of the wind. She stumbled toward us, her wailing like a song:

*Sister-o! Sister! This man did not tell us he was going!*
*God too did not tell us!*
*Have courage! God will explain it all in time!*
*Kofi Ghilchreist, why did you leave us with sorrows?*
*Why did you leave our sister crying? With worries?*

The other women erupted with a low humming. Eurama's body shook with her crying; her body buckled, and she fell into me. Someone pushed a chair beneath me, and she lay across my lap. The woman bent down and took the wrapper tied at Eurama's waist and dramatically wiped Eurama's tears with it. Then she took the edge of the cloth and tied it to the hem of her own wrapper.

"Oh, my dear!" she wailed. "We are here with you. We are here! We are here! Tie your cloth to my cloth. Forget everything. We are here! We will carry this sorrow with you!"

"Twenty-eight years! Even if it is a bad marriage, you will feel it—*paaaaaaa!*" she said quietly to me.

I didn't understand all that was being said, but the absolute power of her promise—that this pain could be bound, that others could carry it, that cloth, the body's second skin, could bear its weight, protect her and us— that, and the fear possessing Eurama's face, convulsed in me and I started to sob.

After a long time, when we'd all fallen again into silence, I heard Eurama's faint voice, teasing, "*Kafo, kafo!* Don't cry, Catherine! Didn't Aunty Mercy say it? And didn't you tell me that you wanted a funeral? And you— you say you're not witchcraft!"

I sat with Eurama and the area women until it was nearly midnight, waiting for Maa Gladys, Eurama's eldest aunt, to arrive from their hometown in the hills beyond Accra. She appeared at the gate in dark mourning cloth, a tall, muscular, black-skinned woman, who despite her age balanced a suitcase and a basket heavy with yams on her head. Others had joined us, sitting in dark-colored *kaba* and slit, black head scarves, and simple slippers, their ubiquitous gold jewelry removed or exchanged for black beads. The power was out again, and we sat under the light of a single kerosense lamp. There was an astounding beauty to the night, with only a small sliver of moon and infinite layers of darkness: skin, cloth, sky, grief manner, death colluding. The world felt steeped in extraordinary power—the depth and the suggestion of something unreachable but elemental to all things. I let the feeling in the yard, the waves of grief, and the power of all of that encircling dark mystery carry me.

A funeral had always been such a vague proposition, even as news came regularly to the shop of people dying. First, it was news of strangers. Then a few weeks before Mr. Ghilchreist's fall, the young man from the house next door had drowned at sea. He had a girlfriend, and his family wanted her to marry the corpse before the burial. It was said that the ghost wouldn't allow her to marry again if she did not prove her love and left his spirit unsatisfied. After weeks of quarrels, and bitter accusations that it was a ploy to get the girl's family to help pay for the burial, he was put in the ground quickly, with little pomp.

Then an old lady began to appear at Eurama's each day dressed in the same mourning cloth, without shoes, her back bent, with hooded eyes. She stood silently at the gate in the mornings until a bowl of rice or *kenkey*, a thick corn paste, was sent to her. She did not appear to be poor; her cloth was clean and neatly pressed, and it was costly. This woman, who I was told was the head of an *esousou*, a traditional women's banking system, was ending a year of widow-seclusion after burying her husband. Custom demanded that she display her grief by putting away worldly things and that she go house to house and accept tithes in her final days of mourning.

"All of the showbiz is over now," Eurama said. "Next two months you will see her walking gorgeously! The first thing she will do is buy blue and white Holland and make a party for thanksgiving."

Mr. Ghilchreist's death seemed almost to have been

ordered. *Obruni, you will meet your indigo*. I felt a pang of guilt, a fear that I had unwittingly summoned or colluded in a sacrifice.

But as the days marched on and the Ghilchreists made plans, there was no sign of blue anything, and my disordered sinking into a shopkeeper's life again seemed to be taking over everything. For the next several weeks, as Mr. Ghilchreist lay in the mortuary, the family consulted those abroad who would send burial money and the senior family members in surrounding villages and towns to set a burial date. Eurama's yard filled with neighbors and others to whom the news had slowly filtered, women from Eurama's and Mr. Ghilchreist's families who out of respect to him, and custom, had closed their shops, handed their children to caretakers, and come to do the work of mourning. With each new presence, Eurama's senior sisters sat reciting the long narrative detailing his death, taking care to show X-rays and lab receipts, to assure everyone that he'd died of pneumonia and not his shameful fall, or the witchcraft of an angry wife or *obruni* who would covet the blue mourning cloths. I would serve drinks to the visitors and nod solemnly when the aunties who passed around and around the X-rays passionately insisted, "Catherine, you are her witness—you were there with the doctor before the man died."

I let the emotion-filled discussions, the bursts of prayer, the endless reciting of costs, wash over me. Each day I made records in my notebook, trying to convince myself that I had not forsaken my work, but the pages were filled with rule after rule directing the ever-tightening noose of Eurama's widow-seclusion.

Things a Widow Can Never Do:

Eat with others; which is the only way a civilized person should eat. *If a married woman eats from the same bowl, she will also lose her husband.*

Eat without a piece of charcoal on your plate. *The charcoal ensures you are really alone. The spirits will never join you.*

Wear nail polish. *Your feet, Aunty! O pe life! You like life! I beg you, remove it, or they will say you killed your husband.*

Touch money. *Me, a widow, with these my five children and two dogs, and my* obruni *who eats meat with every meal. Close my shop for so many weeks?*

Eat for more than survival. *See how your husband is dead and you are growing fat! You must be happy! Or it's true what we hear, that you are making witchcraft?*

Cross the gate and enter the free world. *My dear, don't even sit at the entrance to the gate! Maybe the ghost has gone to Togetherness for a last drink. He will enter the yard, looking for his bed, and meet you there.*

Bathe alone. *Sister-o! The spirit will meet you there! Let me join you in the bathroom so you can be safe.*

Sleep without "high tension" panties, a cloth pulled between the legs and fastened tightly with waist beads. *If you don't the ghost will come to visit that place at night!*

Sleep on your bed just how you like it. *Better you dismantled it, put the mattress on the floor in another corner of the room, so that the ghost is confused and will find another sleeping place.*

The customs, postures of mourning, and labors were endless. But there was not a trace of blue cloth.

"I thought you were studying our cloth," people would say, unaware of the irony, "but it seems you're studying funerals."

I was trying to understand why I felt compelled to stay as each hour marched along. I could beg out of it all, go on with my work, stop by in the evenings. It seemed it was time to step out of Eurama's nest and depend more on my own wit. But a vague sense working through me said there was something important in just sitting still.

One evening, like the first, when we sat in a sea of dark dresses in the yard, just as the night began to fall, I began to make sense of what Eurama and others were teaching me.

"Blue is stronger than black," Aunty Mercy had told me, holding the Dogon cloth against the arm of her house girl, whose skin was dark and poreless, like black porcelain. "One is darker, but in a very dark room, you still can reach out for the walls. The deepest night will be alive with light. The stars are more visible then. Blue-black holds infinity. Blue-black is never done."

"Ah, she is romancing you small-small!" Eurama said.

I was frustrated with the riddle-making. There in the yard, in the encircling dark, as the last bit of daylight fell from the sky, two women plaited Eurama's hair, each taking command over a different sphere, making beautiful order to her head. Others pounded *fufu* and fried fish, drinking Guinness beer. Children squabbled. Others made ready the sitting room where Mr. Ghilchreist's body would be laid for the wake-keeping. An enormous woman entered the gate and stumbled toward us, moaning at the death, nearly tripping over a small child gleefully attempting its first steps.

Indigo mimics and holds all that is in my eye: blackness and light, birth and death, the passages between them. Indigo is not really a color, it is not cloth, I realized. It is only the tangible intangible. The attempt to capture beauty, to hold the elusive, the fine layer of skin between the two.

Death is a praising of life; death teaches us how to live. Color, cloth is simply the praise song.

And so I embraced blackness as my route to blue.

I went to Eurama's house at dawn on the day of wakekeeping. She sat quietly on the veranda, her wrapper draped over her dark-velvet-wrapped head, covering her shoulders. The night before, while the area women had sat in the yard preparing food for the next day's service, Lizzy Hairdresser, Eurama's church sister, had come with a bowl of *lalle*, or henna, and covered Eurama's head with it, dyeing her hair a deep black, appropriate for mourning. Darkened heads were also an ideal of beauty; in the market you could find men and women having their heads blackened for vanity. The thick paste on her head reminded me of an 1832 pencil sketch I'd seen, by the British commander William Allen, of a queen and her entourage in central Nigeria "calling on British visitors." She was kneeling, with her handmaidens behind her, her head covered with a thick paste of indigo and wrapped in white.

The cloth Eurama wore was decorated with a large oxblood-colored skull and bones. *Owuo sei fei.* "Death spoils a house." I recognized it from the Dutch wax seller's shops. Eurama had said it was one of the oldest Dutch wax cloth designs, which meant it could have been traded in West Africa as early as the 1880s.

She seemed to be shivering in the already-rising morning heat. The yard was filled with area women, a somber but spectacular band of decorated blackness, like a flock of exquisite ravens.

I was aware for the first time of Death as something you go and meet. Like a ship, it slips in, laden with its cargo. The band of mourners were like *kayayo* at the harbor, sent to retrieve the family's totaling ache.

"I'm so confused, I don't know my left from my right," Eurama whispered to me at the water pot near the kitchen, where she often went to escape. But during the six weeks since the death, she had run the funeral preparations like the head of a vast corporation. She had defied the restrictions of her seclusion and, because her children were still young, the customary laws that dictated burials as the responsibility of the deceased's children. Everyone had been called from other villages and towns; family had come from Canada, Washington, D.C., Jerusalem, Lagos; the huge burial expenses had been raised; food cooked; funeral *kaba* and suits sewn for four days of ceremony.

And now, hoisting baskets, balancing offerings—the costly items that Mr. Ghilchreist's family elders had requested for the burial—cloaked, too, in blue-black

factory cloths, reminding me of the indigo used to protect
Eurama's money box, her sisters were laughing beneath
their still facades.

"Six bars of Key Soap for one dead body! And how
much cologne?" Eurama kept repeating as we followed
them to the caravan of cars that would carry us to Mr.
Ghilchreist's family house, the expensive half-foot-long
waxy yellow bars sold by Lever Brothers topping their
loads.

Mr. Ghilchreist's mother's house sat on the edge of
Osu, in the old township quarter where Ga peoples had
first settled after migrating from Yorubaland (in what
is now Nigeria) in 1500. Family compounds sat shadowed by Christiansborg Castle, a former slave fort, now
Ghana's White House. We entered a courtyard to a two-
story colonial house, its paint faded and peeling, ringed
by tiny, single-story cement buildings with corrugated
tin roofs and battered wooden doors. It was dawn, but
the air was already thick with heat, charged with expec-
tation and grief.

The house had begun to stir. Women emerged in
wrappers soaked with sweat from the night. Children
stood watching shyly at the edge of the yard. A basket set
down in the compound was overturned by a wild-eyed
cat, who made off with a large smoked tuna until a shoe
was thrown and the fish retrieved from the dusty cement
floor. Eurama sat shrouded on her low stool, in a posture
of total wretchedness, of inconsolance.

As more of a crowd gathered, the eldest Ghilchreist
aunty stood and began to pray. She poured large drops

of schnapps onto the floor, calling to the ancestors. Their spirits should drink and be satisfied and smooth Mr. Ghilchreist's journey to their realm.

The baskets of offerings were placed before Eurama, and without warning the aunties descended on them. They clutched hold of the white dress shirts, the dark suit and underwear and T-shirts, the razors, the hair pomade and satin gloves, the handkerchiefs, the comb and brush, and the large knot of shea butter, displaying them to us before laying them on the burial mat. Their work was exacting, with the vulgar matter-of-factness of a vulture's feeding, their voices cooing, then admonishing, as their hands moved over everything. Eurama and her sisters began to weep as one aunty's litany rose.

She pulled a bowl of tiny, hard limes from the baskets. "Are these for washing the body?" she chided, squeezing one in her hand. She was as tall and cold as a park statue, with a broad, smooth face that seemed barely to move and that betrayed no feeling. She put the lime on the ground and rolled it under her shoe to soften it, then sniffed as she put it back into the bowl.

She moved on to the stack of burial cloths, which would decorate the bed in the room where Mr. Ghilchreist would be laid out for wake-keeping—a display of his wealth and status and family line—before they accompanied the body to the grave. Others would be shared among the mourners.

Eurama and her sisters had spent a few hours unpacking Eurama's cloth boxes in the secrecy of her room. They emerged with some for the extended family to judge: which were appropriate designs, which had the right value to honor the man, which had too much value and should not be squandered. One of her sisters had said something disapproving about the cloths being old, but Eurama had packed them back into the basket with fiery eyes, muttering, "New cloth! With Lady Diana to marry soon and these my five children, a house girl, and two dogs to feed!" In the end, they selected from several of her old *kaba*s. Lady Diana gently undid the stitching in the slits, which had elaborate folding inside so that the full two yards were preserved and sewn but never cut, and then carefully washed and starched and ironed each one with its matching wrapper so that they looked new again.

They were packed into a basket and covered with a heavy blue and white kente, an expensive, elaborately designed hand-loomed cloth once woven with indigo threads and reserved for royals and—as it became a sign of not only prestige but national identity and nationalist pride—slowly adopted by the elite and later those who would afford the several-hundred-dollar cost. Mr. Ghilchreist's cloth was machine woven, most likely produced in a factory in Kenya or China. I'd seen them in the market. They were still costly, but less so than the originals; they represented something modern and prestigious in their own right.

The cloths seemed to meet the Ghilchreist women's approval, and the knot in all of our bodies loosened.

From silver trays we were offered Lipton tea and loaves of French bread slathered with margarine—relative delicacies. The sun was rising fast, and we were growing more uncomfortable under our dark clothing. Eurama sat hunched low, sweat pouring from her chin. There were nearly forty women in the yard now. The aunties were dividing up a bale of coarse fiber used like a loofah that would be used to wash the body. The air was filled with its hay-like dust. A pan filled with small plugs of it was passed among us; we were to take some to also bathe, an act of sympathy and a reminder of death's nearness to our own bodies.

You could feel the grief mounting in the air as the wind carried the threads. Despite the sun, the sky and sea were dark-gray-hued from the Harmattan dust and heavy rains in the night. On the road along the coast, the horizon had disappeared and you could not tell the boundaries between the land and sea and sky. The world became one eternal gray plane. I felt suddenly desperate, caught in the folds of a curtain that would not lift. It was not the curtain of darkness, nor death, nor even grief—these had contours and space and, however wild, a boundary fixed somewhere. The sky seemed to signal a revocation of something, and we were left to turn only to our own bodies, to their blackness, for a landmark.

When we later drove from the aunties' house to the mortuary at Korle-bu Hospital, I stared again, desperately trying to mark the horizon. Then a solitary figure appeared, a man dressed like many weekend funeral-goers in mourning cloth, wrapped in a voluminous toga-like fashion. He marked space and then disappeared again, probably stooping at a place along the shore to empty his bowels.

At the mortuary we walked through a sentry gate into a desolate compound. All at once, summoned by a terrible wailing from behind a cement wall, the yard filled with throngs of women dressed in mourning cloths. A man seemed to sweep the yard, herding the band. SHIT HAPPENS stretched across the chest of his T-shirt, over his rotund belly. Then, as quickly, the women vanished through the gate.

We stood for an hour under a corrugated-tin-covered shed, watching the yard fill and then empty out with each emergence from the mortuary room: a body covered in cloth, carried plainly on a mat to a vehicle holding a coffin.

"Look at your crying face!" I jumped, surprised to hear Eurama's passing whisper. She looked back at me, her eyes twinkling for the first time. She was flanked by Mr. Ghilchreist's aunties, carrying the burial offerings. They disappeared quickly behind the low cement walls of the mortuary building.

The sun beat down on us. I bought chewing gum from the girls milling about selling from head pans and settled into waiting. A giant woman, her body as wide and square as an ice chest, was leaning over the compound wall above us in a frilly-neck funeral *kaba*; she seemed to be surveying the yard with excitement. Indeed, despite the terribleness of that yard, there was an air of spectacle, of morbid entertainment. Under a tree at the center of the yard, a man stood preaching. He moved between Ga and Twi and English.

"Today you have packed your coolers with drinks and food! You are going to enjoy yourselves! See the dresses you have sewn! Ghana, you worship death! You go into a lifetime debt, you spend millions on your funeral cloths and on drink, and you say it is all because you want to see your beloved off, to ensure that their spirit is cared for. You will spend on a corpse, but when your beloved was sick, you waited to send her to hospital! Your own child is at home sick with malaria, and you will tell us that you could not afford to go to clinic, but you will spend your money today, to bury someone! What else is that but worship? And you call yourself Christians. God hates it, and those who do it! Ghana, you worship death!" he exhorted.

A group of women had been huddled to the right of us in a tight circle. I barely noticed, and I missed the import of their gathering until someone moved, breaking the line of bodies, and I realized that they were standing over a small coffin—an unadorned box made from *wawa*, a wood as easy to splinter and pull apart as particleboard. The cover was ajar, and I could see a child's face, smoothed with pomade, a long curl sprung from under a lace-trimmed white hat touching her eyebrow. One of the women standing over her began to wail as the others sent a fire of words to outer provenances, a violent entreaty, imploring the spirit to go and not return, to spare the mother its reincarnation—another pregnancy that might end again in death. The mother of the child lay grief-stricken on the ground at the coffin's side.

An old ambulance from the 1970s, with silver Korean

lettering on the glass, was backing across the yard. As it neared us, I saw that it had been restyled as a hearse, with lace curtains hung in the windows. A security guard ran beside it, corralling the different throngs of mourners, hurrying everyone. The girl's coffin was quickly covered and hammered shut—an act as rough as the woman's exhortations—then was lifted into the hearse; the mourners piled in at either side as the guard barked orders to the driver. The car roared off, with singing and the clanging of a cowbell ringing in the air.

I stood covered with goose bumps in the noonday heat. For several years in high school I had worked in a nursing home, and I was accustomed to death, proud of my command with the washing and dressing of the body. Proud that death did not rattle me. But I had never encountered the body of a child, and somehow the sanitized calm of the institution, the efficient procedure of death, the assumption of a role, helped me through. Here life and death was without boundary, and they seemed to tumble over each other so that I was not sure where one ended and the other began. The mother's crying had stayed with me, and now it became another woman's shrieks. I looked up to see Eurama, standing trancelike at the mortuary door.

The aunties who had followed her admonished her in harsh voices, demanding that she remain in the room, fetch water for his bath, as a wife should, and then hold his feet as the elder women bathed him.

"*Kafo! Kafo!* Don't cry!" one of the aunties barked words meant to soothe. Behind her stood a large public hall with cement slabs that bodies were laid on. I saw Mr. Ghilchreist's bloated corpse being dressed, an open hand, a stiff arm in a black suit sleeve slightly raised, seeming to be waving as he was rocked back and forth with the pulling on of his trousers. A laugh rose in my throat. There was a comedic air about it, death as plain and unworldly as scenes from a Coen brothers film. But it was terrible because it was real.

The yard erupted again as an oil truck drove through the gate, honking so loudly it pierced the ears, a funeral cloth tied across its nose, flags made of the same cloth tied to the antenna. A bus trailed it, the doors snapping open and shut, open and shut, rhythmically. A group of young men alighted. They were clothed in women's dresses, worn inside out with mismatched shoes, dancing wildly as they sang. I'd seen these bands every Friday morning at dawn walking the road. They played cowbells and blew into horns, already drunk on *akpateshie*, a local gin. I was sometimes frightened by their lewdness, their aggression, but the area women all laughed at them. "'Death has confused me,' that is what they sing. That is why they are dressed *baaajaa!*" Lady Diana had explained to me. "They are there to honor death's power over us."

The guards pressed against the crowd again, and we were the ones now being hurried. Lady Diana pulled me along as Eurama's family and the area women rushed to find seats on the bus, leaving space for the next clan of mourners to enter the yard. A coffin lay uneasily propped at the back of the bus, and I was relieved to see that it was still half-covered in brown paper. The body was not there.

But new shrieks erupted, and Mr. Ghilchreist's body, laid on a woven mat, the blue and white kente cloth covering him, the weight of his body causing unsteady hands, was lifted through the back door of the bus onto the last row of seats.

Mr. Ghilchreist's oldest aunty and one of the male elders took posts over the body as we rolled across the yard out into lunch-hour traffic.

We spent two hours on the road from Korle-bu, traversing a wide, stinking sewer, watching men and women urinate there while sheep and goats fed alongside, and traders hawked fruits and bread and plastic wares on the overpasses that straddled it. Enormous oxen en route to the market were herded there to drink.

Eurama rode ahead of us in a car with the aunties. Lady Diana and Kwesi and Christabel rode with me, their foreheads creased with worry and fatigue, their eyes glassy from lack of sleep. The driver had forced everyone to sit and then laid planks across the aisle, creating middle seats. I felt trapped, as sure as the tomb, in this mass of bodies, one dead, the others suddenly revealing the tolls of living and our own mortality. I knew that I could get off the bus, but I was being pulled by a strange momentum, started with my poking into indigo and Eurama's call to me that rainy night.

I was reminded again of the real power of the metaphor of cloth and especially indigo: that it merely materializes the very thin layer between what is seen and unseen, between what can be grasped and what can only be suggested, between the living and the spirit world. I was for the first time not able to assume my own protection. I was not the stranger with the notebook. I was no further from death than anyone.

It took us five hours to travel to all the significant places in Mr. Ghilchreist's life, the places where his spirit was said to linger: the two State Transport Corporation (Ghana's Greyhound) offices in Keneshie in Accra, and Tema, the port city to the west, where he was management; and the Ghilchreist family's modern ancestral homes. At each landmark, the band played louder, the bus and tanker roared from corner to corner of the yard blaring its horn, signaling Mr. Ghilchreist's arrival. Everyone stood crying in the yard as the STC employees filed from their offices to receive schnapps and walk through the bus, paying their respects to the body, while we feasted on oranges and cold drinks and meat pies from the girls selling in the yard.

Finally, we blasted into Osu with the funeral band playing, horns blaring, and a second bus of STC workers. We had to compete for road space with two other area funerals. People had arrived by the carload, and they were making a weekend of it as they went from yard to yard. From my elevated seat I could see over the compound wall into Eurama's house. Eurama was sitting low on a stool on the veranda, dressed now in a flint-black *kaba* and slit. I had been invited by the aunties to help choose it, as well as an anchor cloth for the family, and I'd selected it from the towers of mourning cloths at Makola because it was dark and layered like indigo and its sheen reminded me of the *taglemust*. Something gave way in me when I saw her—an aching tenderness for her body, made vulnerable in the burial rites; the dress, a symbol of my blue passion and the place she'd made for me; and my desire to give her back a dignity and a beauty.

People fell to the ground in grief as the body was taken from the bus. I found myself wailing too.

When I saw the body, laid out in the living room, I was shocked. Mr. Ghilchreist was so bloated that he now looked obese. The autopsy incision curled from his spine to the hairline at his brow. Cotton filled his nose and ears to stop the odors. His lips were sewn, his eyebrows and hair were blackened, and heavy makeup made him appear waxlike. As the body defrosted, his tuxlike suit had been padded with newspaper to absorb the water and to add volume, as ones does when dressing in cloth, to signal prosperity, a body well fed, well clothed. He wore white gloves and jewelry, things he never would have worn alive. The jewelry, which once would have been pure gold—transit expenses to the other world—was made of fool's gold bought at Makola, imported from Dubai or China like most of the mourning cloths.

Beneath him, on a rented brass bed, were layers of expensive black and blue and white cloth, once sure to have been indigos—displays of a well-lived, prosperous, respected life. These cloths lined the bier while the wax cloths Eurama had chosen were tucked beside him, along with *cedi* notes. The living hall was transformed with lace hung from the ceiling, sheets of lace covering the walls where hand-woven prestige cloths would have once hung. There was a red rented floor carpet and plastic flowers in gilded plastic vases. No expense had been spared, relative to Eurama's daily struggle for necessities. To cut back would have jeopardized the dead man's connection with the ancestors; it would have been akin to cutting off some of his air supply.

The man who dressed the body and the room came from a house on Teshie Road. WHATEVER YOU DO, DEATH AWAITS YOU. CONTACT SWEET MOTHER & CO. FOR YOUR BEREAVEMENTS. WE UNDERTAKE THE SALES OF GOWNS, SUITS, WREATHS, MATERIALS, GLOVES, LACE, ETC. the sign board in front of his place read. The dressing had been a task once done by family elders. Ghana indeed had modernized its cult of death; the undertaker had arrived as sure as kente had given way to Lurex threads.

At sundown, people filed into the room to pay respects to Eurama and the aunties before they approached the coffin. The deejay and his sound system orchestrated our grief, playing plaintive dirges, mournful highlife, and American Christian rock. Some of the tears were for hire—women who knew the appropriate gestures, the old dances and postures of mourning, stirring the appropriate drama for a man of Mr. Ghilchreist's stature and for his family, exhausted by more than a month of public grieving.

For hours I sat in the dark in a plastic lawn chair, the ocean breeze blowing cool. A French newscast broke through the pauses in the deejay's playing. I listened to wailing and long conversations with the body:

"Kofi, my dear! You know justice—help me to also know it!"

"You know prosperity. Bless me with the knowledge to also find some."

"Kofi, you were a loving husband, so send a husband to me. I am your daughter-o!"

"Thanks for money still owed, for help in times of need, guidance."

All brought new cries from the mourners.

"*Abussuafo aye ade paa!* The family has tried! *Yen were mfi*, Mr. Ghilchreist *da*. We will never forget you."

"Be off! Leave your wife and stay in your world! Do not trouble her! Protect her and your children!"

"*Kofi! Kofi wou ye ya!* Your death is painful."

"Aunty Eurama! Tie my cloth to your cloth and forget!"

Until the next afternoon, when the body would be laid in the cemetery, the mourners danced and sang, spoke out-sized testimonies in a grand dramatization of Mr. Ghilchreist's life. And there, in a riling sea of decorated darkness, was cloth to help us cope, to comfort our bodies, to summon beauty, to mark our sure existence. I understood now Eurama's riddles: Blue is black. Blue is life, mourning, joy, all at once.

Life and death have exquisite symmetry. The symmetry is held in the color blue. In another time Mr. Ghilchreist's blue kente would have been given to him at the time of marriage, when he became a man and "started life." It, and not the coffin, would have held the body in the grave. The enormous burial customs, the costs, the obsession with beauty and the portage of the corpse are meant to reflect the beauty of the living—the anxieties and dreams and yearnings when life can in fact be so ugly. We are born, we face mortality. What are the mysteries and yearnings in between? Cloth is the portage, the vehicle for the spirit on the irreversible, unsettling march from birth to the grave.

At the center of this grand drama, as we laid Mr. Ghilchreist to rest, I truly learned to see in blue.

After Mr. Ghilchreist had been buried ten days, his soul, it was said, no longer lingered near the body—it had broken free to wander for a year. Eurama's family had packed off, leaving the house in quiet. It was time to venture out. I went in search of Alhaji Ibrahim, one of the well-established antiquities traders in Nima, an old Muslim quarter.

A girl sitting on a stool under the corrugated tin awning of his shop offered her seat to me. "Please, miss, wait small. He dey go come from mosque."

She settled on a mat in the shade, alongside a woman and a bruised and dirt-stained Barbie. Like Barbie, the woman was striking in her improbable build. Her enormous body was neat and surprisingly shapely under her well-starched pink damask boubou. The woman didn't seem bothered at all by her heft; she lay there dramatically at ease. Her face was as large and round as a serving plate. Her head, covered with a sequined blue scarf, lolled in one hand.

The girl began to play. "Rap-unzel, Rap-unzel, drop that your long golden hair," she cooed, twisting Barbie's matted head.

"*Ashawo!*" The woman sucked her teeth.

"Ma!"

"But she is a prostitute! Do you think that the prince would bother to climb something so tall like that and not *jiggy* her?" She spat the skin of the kola nut she chewed and laughed, eyeing my too-short dress.

One of her sherbet-orange mules shoes dropped off, revealing a foot decorated with blue-black geometry. Henna and indigo.

I stared at her foot, and she sucked her teeth and reached for the shoe, letting the plastic snap back against her sole.

A stream of men filed from the mosque into the passageway alongside Alhaji's antiquities shop. Soon Alhaji was standing before me, a tall, broad-shouldered man. His beard, the same white as his *fulan*, hung down to touch the breast of his deep indigo robe. The dye from it leached beautifully into the scarf.

"So you are the *obruni* who killed someone's husband," he said. "I see! And you are done mourning now?" There was a glint of a smile in his eye. "Your friend Ray has told me everything."

Uncle John Ray, an old friend, was an African-American sculptor and photographer who had made his home in Ghana for more than thirty years; he had led me here.

"It is good," Alhaji continued, "because my brother dey go for Mali this week. You dey join; he will take am to Burkina Faso—as far as Ouagadougou. You go find plenty dyers there. See Ray and tell am go call Mrs.

Dagadu. My brother has something to give her; some warthog teeth she wanted. Maybe she go travel with you? I'll expect you both at the STC yard for the Friday bus." He called the girl to serve me a Coke and went to unlock his shop. Men filed in behind him to discuss business, and I left with a nod from him from the door.

Kati Dagadu—I liked her upon meeting her. She had come to Ghana from Hungary before she was twenty, newly married to an older Ghanaian student who was returning home with a degree in petroleum engineering. She had taught herself English in Ghana, had raised two daughters, and had become a master jeweler, running a fashionable boutique, and an expert on the Africa bead trade. Beads and indigo shared a close history and a vernacular, and so we had an immediate bond.

Word was passed back and forth between Uncle Ray and Kati and me. She had decided to accompany me, taking advantage of the chance to travel with a companion while searching for treasures for an exhibit she would curate for a Hungarian foundation.

I said good-bye to Eurama, sad to be leaving her in her quiet house, in the wake of so many hard changes, but she reassured me, "It is time for you to do this now. But be careful of your impatient heart and that stubborn spirit. Don't go by car or lorry. Take STC. Mr. Ghilchreist's spirit will guide your road." She touched the torn strip of one of his burial cloths, tied at my wrist on the day of the wake-keeping for blessing and nearness to him.

When Kati and I went to buy our tickets, a poster in the terminal shed read WE ALWAYS TAKE YOU THERE

ALIVE—TRAVEL BY S.T.C. I felt oddly assured. But on the day we departed, a tall, slender, humorless man arrived. Alhaji's brother seemed displeased, and I wondered if he resented having us along. Then I realized that the boy, no older than fourteen, trailing him too closely, was bound to him at the wrist. His upper-right earlobe had been roughly clipped—the telltale punishment for thievery and a sign to others of a person's bad character.

"*Awo!*" Kati said. "Indentureship, slavery—it hasn't died here-o! Isn't this part of your indigo story? The cloth of royals and slaves. Now you are going to see something! Don't worry-*kra*. You will surely meet your desire."

It was nearing noon, and at the muezzin's call to prayers, most of the other passengers sank into the dust and prayed with the brilliant sun behind them. Kati and I walked to the edge of the yard to rest under a lone cocoa tree. Its leaves were falling, sounding like paper being crumpled and dropped to the floor. The bus yard quieted.

When it was time to board and we took our seats, I knew that I would hold the feelings and memory of Mr. Ghilchreist's corpse in my own body for a long time. He was my unwitting guide.

# Part II

# FINDERS

# FOUR

# The Road to Bobo-Dioulasso, Burkina Faso

We drove through the night, fifteen hours north, to the frontier between Ghana and Burkina Faso, and then on to Ouagadougou to rest before continuing our journey. Bathed in starlight, we traveled long stretches of uninhabited road, interrupted by a few passing vehicles and the occasional glow of lights from low, gentle domes of painted or whitewashed adobe houses that I imagined nested perfectly with the terrain of the moon.

Even at its most desolate, this landscape is ghosted by passages of merchants and traders and people set flowing by centuries of dramatic upheavals—the consequences of wars and extraditions, the sweeping Islamic reform movement, European colonialism, and the trans-Saharan and transatlantic slave trades.

It only took a few hours, the sharing of food, and a stop for prayers to discover that our bus told a modern chapter of this story. There was the boy with the clipped ear and his old Hausa master. Two women with an easy agreement in their bodies—the rare intimacy of co-wives—sat in front of Kati and me in elegant contrast: one was middle-aged, wearing the black cloak of purdah, while the other was in her thirties, her hair fashionably braided, a gold wedding scarf falling loosely over her head and her purple boubou. Their husband sat across the aisle from them, tall and elegant in *taglemust* and a finely tailored blue wool bush suit; a fancy silver pen fastened his UN identification card to his breast pocket. Two teenage girls were traveling home with bright enamel cooking pots, part of their dowry, nested and tied and carefully stowed beside them. A man who had crossed the desert from northern Ghana to Libya, mostly on foot, hoping to find passage to Europe, was now home on leave from college in Egypt and was traveling to see his brother in Ouagadougou. Another who posed as a cattle merchant and had gained entry to Christiansborg Castle, the seat of Ghana's government, for trade hearings, was going home escorted by a customs guard. A woman was traveling in search of artifacts to take to her native Hungary; at a road stop she was met by a trader whom she had summoned with her cell phone; he offered rare Venetian beads and rusted slave manacles. And an American stranger was there, in search of a luminous blue.

I stared into the night, imagining scenes of the past. Indigo had literally helped to pave our road. As early as the fourteenth century, according to Arabic sources, cotton had circulated widely as currency in West Africa. Cloth was measured out and valued in units of length. The practice persists in the *taglemust* and other hand-woven prestige cloths, where strips are made in conventional measures, purchased in a small wheel, and then joined and tailored, their value known and displayed the way Westerners show off luxury labels. From the seventeenth century, caravans traversed the land, one or two thousand persons strong, made up of traders and militia; rich merchant families; pawns, apprentices, and captive persons. Camels carried households, food, and ammunition, ostrich feathers, salt, and gold. On each side of them, in wheels larger than their torsos, dropped below their bellies, was strip woven cloth for dyeing. Indigo was the most valued dye. The caravans often led as many as five hundred slaves at a time—they would become the estimated sixty million humans shipped to the United States, the colonies, and Europe, or to the royal farms of the Ashanti and other industries of African kingdoms and ruling states. In the colonial era, textiles—and particularly indigo cloths—became the largest commodity sold and traded on the West African coast. The colonialist records bear witness: In the 1749 registers of the Dutch West India Company—the largest colonial trade concern for Africa and agent in the slave trade for the Americas—a healthy male slave purchased in Gold Coast (modern Ghana) was worth six ounces of gold, payable in equivalent goods, like a length of cotton cloth.

During the late colonial era and early African independence movements—ushered by Gold Coast in 1957—with the end of interior wars and improved security, transportation, and communications, large caravans slowly became obsolete, and individual traders predominated, using their clan and family members for financing and labor. Yoruba traders from western Nigeria settled in places like Tamale and Yendi in northern Ghana and became dominant in trade by the 1950s. They were often the only resident full-time traders in rural areas neglected by Ghana's southern centers of commercial and political power. Renowned for their quality and beauty, Yoruba indigo woven and resist-dyed cloths circulated widely there, selling for double their Nigerian value.

Until the end of World War I, when inland motor travel increased, lone or small bands of traders cycled on heavily loaded bicycles forty to fifty miles a day to area markets trading indigo. Head porters, paid by the piece, carried spine-twisting loads on twenty-five-to-thirty-day walks to Accra and Tamale from towns like Ilorin in southwestern Nigeria. Indigo had been the backbone of Ghana's northern economy, over time opening avenues for trade in more modern goods like inexpensive, foreign-manufactured electronics. In 1969 an Alien Compliance Act—a punitive law instituted to protect Ghanaian labor interests—forced 200,000 foreign nationals to leave Ghana in two weeks. Yoruba traders and their families were the majority expelled forcibly, leaving everything behind. The depleted landscape through which we drove still bore witness to the resulting economic collapse. When the bus stopped en route, I surveyed cheap poly-ester and cotton cloths hanging in shops where indigo and other Yoruba cloths would have been sold.

We eventually stopped in the city of Salaga for petrol, and I peered into the darkness at the quiet city. For centuries this trade hub had joined markets in Yendi, Mole, and Wa, to the east and west, with those as far as Burkina Faso and probably most notably Nigeria's Hausaland. Salaga had been an epicenter of the trans-atlantic and Saharan slave trades, and the town was rich with reminders: sites of slave markets, the royal palace where the trade was controlled, baths and a sacred tree and other markers where rituals and customs were performed. The trade routes from Salaga to Kano, in northern Nigeria, were among the most important in the early nineteenth century. Kano, the source of the *taglemust*, is one of the oldest and most lucrative indigo dyeing centers in the world and one of the few remaining places where the ancient practices of dyeing are still maintained, though there is daily threat to its collapse.

Tonight the darkness placed a webby veil over what remained of that history, revealing only the bright citadel of the Mobil station and strangers like us, passing on. I tried to quell my hopes of experiencing much more than a tour of history. Would the journey lead me to dyers, to the treasures of old fabled cloths? At times I was no longer sure what I sought. Cloth, certainly, but also something far less tangible: a will to keep a fine blue light, always out of reach, alive in my eye.

The morning after Kati and I arrived in Bobo-Dioulasso, a city one hundred miles southwest of Ouagadougou, on narrow, deeply pitted roads, we rose early and set off walking, guided by the minaret of the ancient adobe mosque, its dark-sticks foundation poking through the white-washed adobe like many wonderful high-tuned antennae. As we walked, we saw blue wrappers peeking from under hemlines of boubous, light blue damask dresses with indigo bled into the bottom quarter of the hem, and I was bursting with excitement. Eurama's spirit reached my ear, whispering, *"Are these the Beautiful Ones? Don't rush!"* I tried to slow my heart, to calm the voyeur's eye that I fixed on the women's underskirts, taking measured steps beside Kati as we played a game of "I Spy," peering coyly into the gates of compounds as people alighted and disappeared along the road.

At one house, a man stood propping open a green metal door, surveying the street. Behind him a young girl stood with a bucket of water on her head. Her back was to us, and she was talking to someone, gesturing with her free hand, until she turned and walked out of our frame. A skein of inky blue threads hung in her place on a tree branch, a clay dye pot planted where her feet had been.

Just inside the gate we met Madame Harouna, a bent-over doyenne with a sorceress's hands colored blue to her wrists. She quickly retreated to her house, where she traded her stained work clothing for a blue-and-gold-satin scarf tied tightly on her head, covered with a white lace *miafi* that fell over the shoulders of a purple and green tie-dyed-damask dress. I could see right away that she was a mischief-maker. She seemed amused by our visit, by my wild, obvious thirst, by the frenzy in the young men in the yard. Her son, eager to show us the ground loom on which he worked, was weaving a cover from threads dyed in three shades of indigo that were stretched many feet across the compound. The others sat idle until they found reason to jump hungrily to negotiate the Wangara she spoke and our poor French, acting as go-betweens. We couldn't express much, so exhausting was the jostling, the translations. Finally she grasped my hand with her aged blue palm and led me to her dye pots, stooping to stir them, allowing the dye to trickle onto her finger and then tasting it with a chef's scrutiny.

I peered into the pot at a treacly, pungent blue bath of rainwater and ash, urine, and tiny fermented leaves. I wanted to throw myself in.

It was not the first time I'd encountered an indigo dye pot.

"A crazy idea—a North American dye pit," my professor had said in his offhanded way when I had told him I had a bowl of the pounded and dried leaves of Ibadan indigo in my kitchen. I wanted to try to make a dye vat, knowing that because I was not an initiate in the tricky science and cosmology, it would fail as anything more than a place to dream.

I had just returned from an artist's indigo studio in St. Helena in the South Carolina Sea Islands. A South Carolina poet had told me about it when I'd talked about wanting to write about indigo at a conference we attended. The studio was run by a woman, Arianne King Comer, a native of Detroit. Arianne had traveled to Turkey and parts of Asia to study natural dyes and eventually traveled to Yorubaland. She had become obsessed with indigo and made the connection with the indigo plantations in the South Carolina Sea Islands that her ancestors had worked on. She had set up a studio there and brought over some Yoruba dyers to restore the African connection to an American legacy.

At Arianne's, I found three red clay pots filled with *indigofera* dye from Ibadan, steeped in the laterite earth behind her studio. With the red dirt, the water tanks, the low cement house with plantain growing in the yard, the birds and dogs wandering in and out of rooms, it could have been Nigeria. I stayed for a few days, lucky to arrive when one of the vats was matured for dying.

With a few yards of white cotton cloth, I entered the dye pot's magic. The first time the cloth was submerged below the thick, foamy, oily head of the bath and then quickly released, it emerged a thin, dirty yellow. The color was so weak that I imagined it spoiled, but as I shook it in the air, the yellow darkened and changed cast. With each submersion and each infusion of oxygen, the cloth transformed from the yellow hues of skin through a spectrum of greens into watery blues that progressively deepened. The skein of threads hanging on the branches of the tree shading us, bleeding blue into the earth, were as dark as the Yoruba indigo I had at home.

Here at Madame Harouna's, for the first time the dye pot was not academic. It felt familiar. And it felt holy, like a shrine. I was content to just be there, without asking what cloth, what use, what meaning or history, simply knowing the place in my senses.

The dye pot was aging, she had told me. The color she could achieve was weakening. She would not start a new dye pot again until she'd amassed more orders. There was little demand for indigo, and the work was consuming. Her children did not share the passion. There was little I could do there but look and feel.

The young men had drawn back from me, but I could see them calculating my gaze at a lovely woven wrapper—three dark shades of indigo joined by white bands—that they'd hung on a branch of the tree. Of course I would buy it.

When Kati and I left Madame Harouna's with the wrapper, and her address tucked in my bag, I was eager to resume our playful hunt. There was much more to discover, I was sure. But as soon as we stepped through the gate we could feel the mood on the street had changed. We saw a large crowd of young people moving toward the house. We could feel the tension in their bodies, a kind of contained frenzy, until—in a moment—they broke into a run, coming at us like frightened deer.

Madame Harouna's gate had latched behind us. We pushed and pounded, and by the time the hollow echo of our hands on the iron summoned her, men who looked like ordinary citizens with thick rubber crops were chasing the crowd. She opened the gate, hurried us into her yard and slammed it shut. I didn't understand why she was laughing as she led us to the latrine at the side of the compound. Doubling as a bathing place, it was a roofless adobe closet with a small stinking pit at the center, set with a porcelain toilet cover over which you squatted. The smell of feces vaporizing in the 104-degree heat was overwhelming.

The ground at the edges of the latrine was sloped, and the mud wall had eroded and broken away so you could easily peer over it unseen. In spite of the smell it was a perfect lookout point. She motioned to us to watch the crowd advancing along the road. The men descended on them, the slap of their crops setting them running again.

"*Mort*," Madame Harouna choked.

Someone had just died? Were others going to die with them? Were we in danger? I felt my bowels slip. Madame Harouna was still laughing.

By now the crowd was wheeling back, recircling, and people were jeering as it grew. Some made playful taunts. I noticed then that there were many small children among them, squealing with excitement.

Her son explained over the wall that a funeral procession was assembling. One of the masqueraders, an old master from an important secret society, had died. Young people were losing respect for the masquerade, the son explained, and the beatings were meant to reinstill respect for its seriousness and power.

"When they bury the man, you will see the finest indigo!" he said.

*For now*, there was no sign of masks, no indigo, only the men with crops and boys with slingshots, and crowds of young men and women in jeans making sport on the road.

We stayed at Madame Harouna's until the streets quieted. Later that evening, as the sun was setting, I walked from the mosque, toward our host's house, and wondered about my remove from everything. Kati and I had discovered little of what the morning promised. No other dyers, no funeral procession, none of the treasures we sought. Just a lovely, sleepy town that featured a well-stocked library, a shop selling fresh-made gelato, and a cinema that regularly screened not the usual fare of popular grade-B movies but African art house films.

We stood in the streets looking simultaneously at things ancient and avant-garde, expecting our desires might finally be met, but what we both hoped to discover still felt so out of reach.

"Is indigo really to be found?" I asked Kati.

"You will find it! But it is left for you to answer if indigo is a cloth or a lesson in life's mysteries discovered from a latrine," she giggled. "For me, I have found the rarest, the most beautiful beads. I keep some for my collection, but I put many one by one into a string for someone to wear, for my mother-in-law to add to someone's ceremonial this and that, or to give out to a visitor—someone like you, whose spirit for this world is strong. For me it is not the accumulation of the beads, it is the accumulation of so much history with others, a marking of passages, so much shared. It's not the beads but the life they represent that accumulates on a fantastic strand! But don't mistake me-o! I also like fine-fine things!"

"Ehhhhh-heeee!" she said. "Now decide!" We had turned a corner, and I had not been looking, but before us was a woman sitting on a mat in front of a house. Her legs were outstretched, her braided hair was uncovered, gold jewelry glinted from her ears and neck, and she wore a crisp pinstripe blouse and indigo *ikat*—one tied at her waist, one over her shoulder in the fashion of younger women. Beside her were two small girls, their necks freshly powdered after their evening bath, adorned only in gold earrings, amulets at the infant's wrists, and strands of tiny white waist beads.

It was Baule cloth from Ivory Coast, I knew, recognizing the elaborate *ikat* designs with stark blue and white contrasts and touches of bright reds and greens and yellows. The indigo came from the legendary Dioula dyers from more northern reaches—famous also for weaving, as Koranic scholars, and as long-distance traders—who tie-dyed the threads used in the blue warp.

I stopped, calculating in my head, and out loud with Kati, if I should approach her. All the while Eurama chided in my ear, "*Catherine, don't disgrace yourself!*" Just then it began to pour violently. Everyone scrambled for cover, and Kati and I found ourselves being led by the woman into a bedroom, where we sat in total darkness, cozy among stacks of dowry pots, trunks, and clutter, amid the bodies of others we could not make out. The rain fell for a long time before someone entered with a kerosene lamp, and everyone loosened into conversation.

I asked the woman about her cloth. She shrugged, uninterested. Then one of the men in the room—always, because they were first to be schooled, our French-speaking emissaries—calculating, in the way I was calculating, a coup of some sort—prompted her. "You want to buy this," he said. It was not a question. The man left, came back, and left again after speaking to her in Wangara. Then came a phone call and a message.

Someone's sister who lived in town had purchased some of the cloth on credit. The finer pieces were expensive commissions, but she could no longer pay the woman

*Les amazones et le chacha.*

Dahomey Amazons ca. 1890 in woven indigo cloths.
*Photo by Edward Foa, courtesy of the Getty Research Institute.*

Nike Davies Okundaye.
*Photo courtesy of
Nike Davies Okundaye.*

Indigo dye pots at Nike Art Center, Oshogbo, Nigeria. *Photo courtesy of
Nike Davies Okundaye.*

Malinke dyers in the Futa Jallon region of Guinea. The woman on the left is beating a cloth to give it a finished sheen. Vintage postcard. *Photo by Edmund Fortier ca. 1910. Collection of Duncan Clarke.*

Jan Fentener van Vlissingen (right), then general manager and part owner of Vlisco, and Cees Krantz (leaning), head of design department, visiting traders in West Africa, 1964. *Photo courtesy of Vlisco BV.*

THIÈS. - Dame Ouolof

Hartmann, édit., Thiès

A Mali woman in indigo finery ca. 1974. "Une Amoureuse de Thé" by Malick Sidibe. *Courtesy of the Jack Shainman Gallery.*

A Wolof woman from Thiès, Senegal, ca. 1910, wearing cloth with a Wolof/Portuguese/Japanese/Islamic heritage. Vintage postcard. *Collection of Duncan Clarke.*

Aboubakar Fofana in his Bamako, Mali, studio, removing indigo cloth from the dye pot after several submersions and watching the color magically deepen as it is infused with oxygen. © 2003 by Francois Goudier.

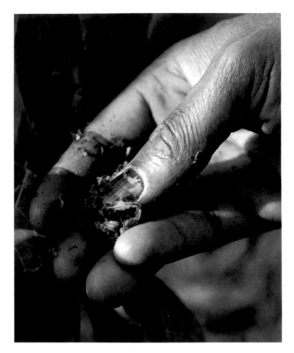

Young indigo leaves crushed in hand of Aboubakar
Fofana, Bamako, Mali. © *2003 by Francois Goudier.*

*Adire* sellers at Oje Market, Ibadan, Nigeria. © *1971 by John Pemberton III.*

Mercy Asi Ocansey in her shop in Accra, Ghana, 1999. *Photo courtesy of Mercy Asi Ocansey.*

Susanne Wenger (Àdùnní) at her home in Oshogbo, Nigeria, 2000. *Photo by Catherine E. McKinley.*

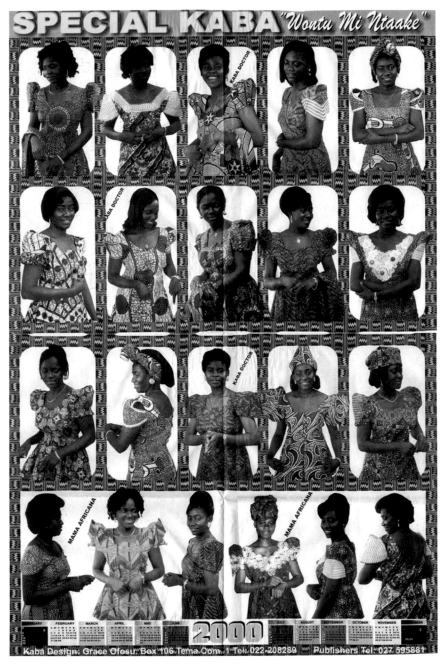

*Kaba* and slit style chart, Accra, Ghana. *Collection of the author.*

Detail, Vlisco wax cloth. *Collection of the author.* © *2010 by Michael Chuapoco.*

Detail of the indigo dye pot symbolizing the reign of Dahomey king Dako Donou (1620–1645) on a contemporary Fon appliqué cloth. *Collection of the author.* © *2010 by Michael Chuapoco.*

1

2

3

4

5

MAMA

6

GAWANIOOTEPE

GUARANTEED DUTCH WAX    VLISCO

7

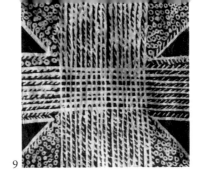

8

9

VERITABLE WAX HOLLANDAIS    VLISC

GUARANTEED DUTCH WAX    VLISCO

10

11

12

1 and 2. Details of vintage Yoruba *adire* cloth. 3. Detail of vintage cloth acquired by the author in St. Louis, Senegal. 4. Detail of Yoruba men's shirt with embroidery. 5. Detail of vintage Yoruba *adire* cloth. Many women and girls who designed these cloths were illiterate and the meaning of the words inscribed here is unknown. 6 and 7. Details of a Vlisco wax cloth introduced for Mother's Day 2010 that is a tribute to Mama Benz, the legendary cloth traders of Togo. 8 and 10. Details of a contemporary Vlisco print that has traces of the original patterning of cloths intended for trade with colonial Indonesia. "Java" prints are still beloved in Ghana and are an elite category of Dutch wax cloths. 9. Detail of vintage Yoruba *adire* cloth. 11. Detail of vintage Yoruba *adire* quilted by the author. 12. Detail of Yoruba men's *agbada*, a robe, featuring embroidery and *ikat* patterning, both symbols of prestige. *All cloths from collection of the author.* © 2010 by Michael Chuapoco

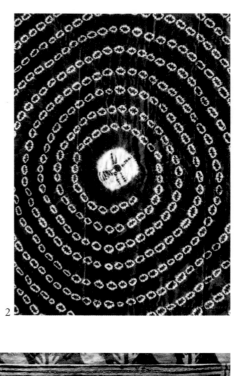

1 and 2. Detail of vintage Yoruba *adire*.
3. Detail of vintage Yoruba *adire* brocade cloth. *All cloths from collection of the author.*
© *2010 by Michael Chuapoco.*

Indigo dye pots and dyed threads drying in Madame Harouna's compound, Bobo-Dioulasso, Burkina Faso. *Photo by Catherine E. McKinley.*

Fulani men in Agadez, Niger, wearing Kano indigo. Indigo-dyed ostrich feathers adorn the hat. *Photo by Catherine E. McKinley.*

Tuareg woman in Kano indigo at a wedding in L'Aïr Massif, Niger. *Photo by Catherine E. McKinley.*

A queen and her entourage calling on British visitors, Central Nigeria, 1832–33. "Her hands and feet were deeply tinged with henna . . . her hair—thickly plastered with indigo—was enveloped in a soft turban." From William Allen, *Picturesque Views on the River Niger*, 1840. *Courtesy of the Library of Congress.*

Ohori-Yoruba woman with tattoo-scarifications wearing *adire* indigo wrapper.
© *1973 by Henry John Drewel.*

it belonged to, who would be coming from Abidjan again that month. That someone was Sophie; she could be found selling fish in the night market.

I thanked them for the tip, and Kati and I went back to our host's house in the slowing rain and encroaching darkness.

I left Kati at a *pito* bar, a place that served local millet beer, near the house, and rode with our host's son, Aziz, on a motorbike through muddy pot-holed streets, from one spot to the next in search of the fish seller Sophie. We finally found her stand, but she had gone home; there was no market in the rain. Another young woman had taken over; we were shown the path to Sophie's house.

Sophie greeted me with amusement and went to bathe, returning in an indigo boubou for the occasion. The cloth would cost twenty-three CFA francs, quite a lot, of course, she said, but it was not there with her—it was at her sister's house. We waited while she carefully arranged her hair and summoned another bike; then we rode back to her spot in the market to wait for her and preserve Aziz's last bit of petrol.

Sophie retrieved a key from under the tray that she sold her fish from. She collected my money, then rode off, leaving me with Aziz there at the roadside long enough that I felt like we'd been fooled.

Kati's words echoed. Was it the cloth or the experiences that were really what was precious?

Later, at the *pito* bar, under the spell of the rain and four *balafons*—long resonating instruments like

xylophones with calabashes strung on their under-
sides—I shared one of the wrappers with Kati like
spoils of war while Aziz grumbled about the price
of the cloth, that it was not at all fine. No, it was
not as fine as the first cloth, but it was still lovely
somehow, with a softness and the rich color of fading
blue-black denim. We bought the dancers a calabash of drink in celebration of a day of riches. They
moved furiously in a fierce birdlike dance, until they
became entranced and seemed near to lifting from
the ground. We let the slow drizzle soak us until the
band broke for the night. Then we walked home and
dragged our mattresses outside to sleep under the
metal awning and a quarter moon.

Someone pulled a TV outside, and it whirred to life.
Others gathered to watch the French news broadcast.
Ouagadougou was wracked with protests and car burn-
ings after a failed inquiry into a journalist's death. We
were heading back to Ouagadougou the next day to rest
and buy the things needed to begin the long journey
home. We'd journeyed for thirty-two hours from Accra
and now had the return journey ahead of us. It made
little sense, to come so far and never stay long enough
to do more than dance along the world's surface. What
could I really know of indigo? What could I know about
anything? But as I lay on the edge of sleep, I felt content
somehow for the first time. Kati's question had offered
me clarity.

I heard the slap of leather slippers on the hard earth,
the clank of iron, the sound of someone's retreat. Then

the whirring of a fan began, blowing air across our bodies. The air blew too cold, and yet without the fan the air was stifling. Kati and I reached for our indigo wrappers to cover our bodies. What wonderful decadence!

# FIVE

# The Chanel of Africa, Ghana

The Ghana Textiles Printing (GTP) plant is housed in a building of Dutch modern design, erected from imported steel and concrete by Vlisco, its parent company in the Netherlands. It is a modest building, yet it is grand relative to most of the other industrial compounds of Tema, a port city sixteen miles west of Accra that grew up around a man-made harbor built in the 1960s in the optimism of the early years of independence.

I decided to visit the plant to try to learn more about wax cloth and the Dutch relationship to indigo.

Eurama and I sat on cool cement benches at the factory entrance alongside men policing a sophisticated security gate. It was her first venture out since Mr. Ghilchreist's burial. She had been reluctant to journey out but was relieved to escape the house and so many watchful neighbors. She dressed in her plainest, most staid black *kaba*, but when we sat down, she exchanged her simple, well-worn slippers for black sequined ones and powdered her face. European men hurried past in slacks and crisp white shirts, their faces ruddy, sometimes blistered from the sun and heat. Ghanaian men emerged from a doorway, refastening their company-issued overalls after being searched, and the speed and tension in their exits reminded me of Richard Wright's chronicles of the gold mines in *Black Power*, his odd tome of what he called "reactions" to Ghana at the moment of independence.

It seemed to me that cloth would be difficult to boost; any amount less than the six yards required for *kaba* and slit, or a man's traditional togalike attire, would have no real value and was akin to having a pocket of torn bills. I later learned that Dutch technical knowhow was what was most carefully guarded, and that cloth designs too were protected with the fierceness of European couture houses. A tiny swatch or a digital file was all that was required to rapidly reproduce cloths in other African or Chinese or Indian factories, whose agents would then flood the African markets with cheap imitations.

We sat for a long time in the heat and noise of the GTP plant. There was a dizzyingly sweet and acrid bruise to the air. It was a familiar scent, and I struggle to place it.

A transistor radio hummed alive beside us: "*Dr. Abalaka, a Nigerian medical doctor outside of Abuja, claims to have a vaccine for HIV/AIDS. He's injected himself six times with the AIDS virus and the vaccine has protected him. That act alone, he says, is 'absolute scientific proof' of his claim. The government is staging a review and is withholding comment, but hundreds of government soldiers are going to him and paying close to $1,000 U.S., selling everything they have to receive treatment. International pharmaceutical companies are apparently curious. The doctor says it would be 'unpatriotic' and 'unethical' to reveal any details until he has the president's full support and recognition . . ."*

I was feeling overpowered by the heat and the smell, and the news report, betraying neither doubt nor irony, seemed bizarre and otherworldly. Then my memory was moved.

When I was in college at Sarah Lawrence in the late 1980s and involved in pan-Africanist cultural organizations, I had made a trip with friends who were dancers and artists to a warehouse several hours away in New Jersey to buy the best-quality African cloths, which were not readily available even in New York. At the warehouse young white women who worked for Dutch and British companies were overseeing stacks of twelve-yard pieces of wax cloths packed into shelves in polyurethane sleeves. The plastic and dye smells sickened me, and the whole thing was disturbingly un-African. The salesgirls were most accustomed to filling mail orders to shop owners in Texas and Boston. They had no particular love for what they were selling; they could have been working for Kmart or a textbook company. In those environs, the beauty of the cloths seemed diminished, and as we added money together so that we could meet the thirty-six-yard purchase minimum, I felt suddenly reluctant. But we were buying the cloth primarily for the memorial service of a dancer friend who had died of AIDS.

Far from the warehouse, the smell became more gentle and life was breathed into the cloth by the bodies it adorned. It was as if by literally touching the flesh the cloth became charged, like a fetish object.

What was that smell? I was encountering it again.

My thoughts were interrupted as we were summoned

to an office. There the Executive Madame, a large woman with a stern beauty, her permed hair slick with oil, sat behind a large wooden desk in an outdated blue corporate skirt suit. She was reading the introductory information I'd been asked to prepare and present at the guard station. It was really only a short prospectus for my Fulbright research and a résumé, so I watched her long scrutinizing gaze, her painstaking attention, certain that she was not reading a thing.

When she got up from her desk, she moved silently around the office, opening various cupboards and document binders. After a long while she cleared her throat.

"GTP strives for beauty in its cloth," she said in a voice heavy with the sweet, nasally tonals of Twi. "Vlisco is the Chanel of Africa. You could say we are the Calvin Klein, the Yves St. Laurent, the Gucci too."

She seemed to sniff as she surveyed my dress made up of one of Aunty Mercy's batik cloths. "Wax cloth will be boring for you. And after all, this is just a plant. There is very little to see. Indigo was always used, but our new collections are changing. Ghanaian women like modern things. We are using more browns and greens; we are moving into many other colors too."

She handed me some promotional postcards, of women in couture-styled bright cloths with backgrounds of baobab trees and African sunsets. I'd shopped in Woodin, Accra's fanciest boutique, also owned by Vlisco, that carried similar expensive ready-made designs. I was mesmerized and also made uneasy by the catering to assumed tastes. The "latest" designs featured the symbol for the newly minted

Euro and computer mouses and refrigerators and fans—consumption desires beyond most Ghanaians' reach.

"The local dyers—these petty-petty craftspeople—are not really doing indigo dyeing anymore either, but at least they will provide you a quaint study. Women with babies at their backs, native scenes."

She had been pulling pages from the binders and file drawers as she talked and, one by one, calling for a secretary to come for them. Now she handed me the secretary's copying and another little pack of the postcards. She stood sizing me up, trying to make sense of the young American "student" (I'd found it a useful pose) with Ghana connections (the visit had been arranged by a "big man," a prominent friend of Mr. Ghilchreist's brother) and U.S. embassy sponsorship.

"But perhaps I can make steps with the higher administrators if you'd like to know more," she said with the suggestiveness and direct glance that were a cue for bribe giving. In that moment, we both began measuring the stakes, tightening our game face.

I told her I'd call on her again, not sure that I would.

As we walked down the long corridor, she acknowledged Eurama for the first time. "Aunty, sorry-eh? Sorry. Your husband? But Aunty, your shoes . . ."

By now the factory smells seemed more piercing.

"What is that smell?" I asked.

"It is your indigo—but of course we use an industrial dye—and trichloroethylene, something used to remove the resin from the cloths after the dyeing process."

I was familiar with trichloroethylene. In Attleboro,

where I grew up, there had been worries about the local mills along the Bungay River dumping the compound. It was known to contaminate water supplies and cause respiratory, nerve, kidney, and heart damage with prolonged exposure. What of Tema water and soil, and what of the workers? What of those who wore the cloths?

"She should satisfy herself!" Eurama said as soon as we were out of earshot, sucking her teeth, and letting her shoes clack harder on the floor. "What at all did this woman do for you? Shame! Working for the white people in big big offices and still as hungry as a lion, asking for bribes!"

I looked at the pages that the Madame had copied for me. There were images of African women, dressed in Vlisco sewn in elegant *kaba* and slit, posed examining cloth on industrial rollers. I would have liked to imagine these women were friends of Aunty Mercy during her stint in Holland. They would run the offices, lunch together, and go home to their Dutch husbands, their work a respite from housewifery.

"Dog labor!" Mercy had said of her days at the plant. "There are no proper jobs for Africans there." I thought about the Executive Madame's patronizing of me. In Mercy's own factory in Teshie-Nungua, on the road to Tema, she was not at all a quaint figure but a woman in splendid hand-printed batik and vintage Chanel sunglasses, driven in her shiny American pickup truck, her bag stuffed with more bills than the Madame would ever have earned. In Ada, her hometown, she held a title in an important traditional council that had power with the national government.

The other pages contained photos of large industrial indigo vats, fashioned as deep, low-lying troughs with twelve wheels—resembling enormous film reels—suspended above, cloth spun around them seeped with indigo. The photo was a surprise; the wheels were so eerily reminiscent of the ancient means of transporting cloth on camels. At the same time, it disturbed my image of small clay dye pots, or even the larger pits like those of Kano that were deep wells in the ground, which required taxing handwork, craftsmanship, months of toil, a culture of patient caretaking and ritual akin to, if not actually part of, the devotion of shrine-keeping. It was, for me, an act of looking simultaneously forward and backward along a deep schism that I wanted to trace. The material she'd given me hinted at a surprising history, and as I later journeyed closer to the ancient practices, I kept being pulled back to the history of Vlisco.

On the way home from Tema, I convinced Eurama to stop for ice cream. "Only if we hide ourselves," she said. "A widow can't eat ice cream."

We found a corner table near a window at the top of Frankie's, a Lebanese-owned restaurant frequented by expats, where few would recognize Eurama's status or care. Across the street was the Woodin boutique, its shiny storefront filled with ready-to-wear designs mixing the blue and white Vlisco cloths—the old, esteemed designs customarily worn for funerals and church ceremonies and baby namings—with denim and silvery embellishments.

Aunty Mercy's shop was less than two hundred feet up the adjacent street. The contrasts in African and Dutch modernities, as dramatic as those reminiscent images of the ancient and industrial wheels, were so powerful, I knew that I needed to understand them before I again ventured out.

I went back to the university library to try to understand what the Vlisco literature had suggested. And this is the story that I found:

The Dutch flag had flown in the Gold Coast as early as 1594. By the 1800s, English, French, and other European rivals occupied forty fortifications along the four-hundred-mile coast, used partly as trading posts and bulking and distribution centers for ivory, gold, hides, gum, spices, and slaves. The Netherlands became the fourth-largest slave-trading nation, following England, Portugal, and France, exporting a recorded 477,782 captives between 1630 and 1794. Dutch textiles had made up 57 percent of the goods exchanged for human lives. In fact, by the late 1600s, cloth constituted more than 50 percent of European exports to West Africa on a whole. Record after record show African lives being traded for two or four "measures"—likely two or four yards of cloth, each two-yard piece the length of an African woman's wrapper. At the same time American abolitionists and Quakers staged boycotts of indigo and cotton cloths to further their antislavery efforts. In the 1800s Dutch colonialists in Indonesia, recognizing the beauty and profitability of Javanese batik cloths (which were widely believed to have originated in India long before Christ and were introduced to Indonesia and Malaysia around 1275 by the Chinese), studied batik processes, hoping to enter the trade. In cities like Helmond in the southern Netherlands, where Vlisco had been established, the Dutch successfully industrialized batik. These factories were already producing "blue cloths," iconic blue-and-white-patterned textiles dyed originally with woad, Europe's indigenous blue dye. The process of printing blue cloths was similar to the base process for industrial batik.

In the late 1800s Dutch merchants introduced a less costly product to Indonesia that they hoped would undercut the local market. Indonesians immediately rejected the Dutch cloths, preferring their own hand-patterned, wax-resist designs. The Dutch process relied on resin in lieu of wax, as it was more suitable to the European climate and combined better with the dyes. The combination of resin and nonindigo dye created half-tones and crackling lines in the cloths instead of the bold, exact lines and color contrasts typical of Indonesian batiks. Indonesians regarded these qualities as imperfections, and the Dutch market failed.

The Dutch fleet of the British-owned East India Company—which was the most significant colonialist agent in Asia, administering governments and militias and trading in silks, opium, tea, indigo dyes, and other goods—was by then making regular stops at stations along the Gold Coast en route to and from Europe.

The Dutch soon discovered that West Africans favored the cloths that the Indonesians had eschewed.

Indigo cloths were already one of the most highly valued trade items. The dark blue base design in many of the cloths was attractive; and—particularly when smaller, repetitive patterning was used—the cracklings and dye tones created a kind of movement in the cloth and body similar to the beauty of indigenous African cloths.

Living in the shadow of Elmina Castle, the first European building south of the Sahara, built in 1482 by the Portuguese and then occupied by the Dutch (and now a UNESCO World Heritage site for its importance in the transatlantic slave trade), was a small community of former Dutch army conscripts who had served in Indonesia. These men, part of three thousand "Donko" slaves—the lowest caste of captives of the Ashanti empire—were sent to Indonesia from 1810 to 1840 under a system of de facto slavery. These men eventually bought their freedom with army service and resettled in Elmina beginning in the 1820s in a close-knit community of relatively elite "Old Javanese" pensioners. They flew the Dutch flag, spoke Malay as a common language, and put themselves at the disposal of the governor, making expeditions into the interior. They dressed in Javanese cloths; the wrapped and togalike draped clothing of Akan men of the Gold Coast was not too dissimilar from Indonesian dress styles. These men's lives have been little documented, but they are also partly responsible for Vlisco's influence in West Africa.

The slave trade effectively ended in 1841, persisting for thirty years after its abolition under the 1814–15 Vienna Congress. Profits from the colonial cloth trade had nonetheless grown so significant that the market persisted long after the abolition of slavery. By 1876, when Vlisco began formally shipping cloth to the Gold Coast and concertedly pursuing an African market, they were extending the profits from goods that had long been exchanged and stored alongside captives in the holds of the coastal forts. Inside of Elmina Castle, the wrought-iron railing to the main building bears a W, presumably for King William I, the Dutch king who sponsored the three factories that were the backbone of the Indonesian cloth trade, eventually inherited by Vlisco. Knowing this history put a new order to my way of seeing.

In the 1920s and 1930s Vlisco began a process similar to the Indonesian one with West African cloth designs. These cloths often incorporated traces of Indonesian designs, and "Java" designs themselves became an expensive category of Vlisco cloths sold in Africa.

In the Woodin window there was also a display of neon pink and blue and red "Angelina," the iconic, usually dark green dashiki cloth emblematic of 1960s and 1970s Black and African identities and Black liberation struggles throughout the globe. It long predated the daishiki era and was one of the earliest "Java" prints to be traded; ironically, the design had been inspired by Coptic patterning.

I kept thinking about Ghanaian women's dresses and the "100% Guaranteed Real Dutch Wax" stamp on the selvage, always—until the late 1960s, when sepias and other colors were introduced—a crackling line of beautiful blue. Most women choose to display this selvage rather than fold if into their hemlines. Some of the most expensive "Super Wax" cloths even feature the Vlisco logo as centerpieces to their designs. I had once read about an Alabama slave owner, a man named T. H. Porter, who made his chattel wear buttons with his name stamped into them. Buttons—much less custom designs—were such a relative luxury in Porter's era, and slaves were afforded few or none. The arrogance of this requirement, the sick vanity, always stayed with me.

Ghanaian and other West Africans wear colonial and slave history in bright, intoxicating displays every day. In fact, the very measure of the cloth evokes the measure of a captive person's life.

# six

# Amazons, Wives of the Gods, and Mama Benz, Ghana/Togo/Benin

In Irving Penn's lens, the daughters of the Mino, the legendary Amazon women warriors of the ancient kingdom of Dahomey (the modern country of Benin), stare into the camera with a watchfulness of women beyond their years. They are lithe, their bodies on the meridian of pubescence, their breasts taut and bared of everything but collars of powder—a cosmetic, with spiritual purpose too—appointed with thin coral and gold and metal necklaces. The heavily cicatrized bodies of some of the girls mark their clan, their status, and their various initiations; the fresh wounds were likely rubbed with a mix of henna and indigo to deepen their relief against the skin. Their bodies are wrapped gloriously in indigo cloths designed with chieftaincy leaves and scar-like lines and patterns like sugar cubes. The cloths were ironed or beaten on a wooden block by a wooden mallet, until they achieved a starchy crispness and sheen. The girls sit as if in ritual as much as studio scene. Their heads, tied in wax cloth and satin, disturb the palate of blue and white and black, with a sudden flash of red or gold.

The photos appeared first in *Vogue* magazine in 1967, when Penn journeyed with his ambulant studio on special assignment to Dahomey. The girls' faces are arresting; so much feeling moves behind their impassive stares, and the cloth absorbs every mood, projects it as a fiercely playful theater. It is character acting. Penn admits that the photos he took are a creation of "extreme artifice": the bodies are in studied poses, recast in startling relief against a stark white studio backdrop.

I find the photos troubling for their exoticism, for the way the girls were sexualized, and yet I realize their power, because the girls' eyes and the way the cloth was photographed lived on in my imagination. One morning I woke up thinking of the images, and I decided to travel to Benin to see if I would find something to supplant them; bits of blue sugar cubes and leaves. I also thought of the journey as a kind of dry-run to Nigeria, which was just a few hours beyond Porto Novo, a chance to test the infamous road and border crossings through Togo and Benin, to see if I was ready for the indigo badlands, the place from which Fulbright had revoked its grants.

The next day I was leaving Accra in an ancient Peugeot at breakneck speed, the road below exposed through the rusting carriage. I sat in a middle seat between a woman with baskets of dried fish and yam at her feet and a Cameroonian student returning home on vacation.

You won't travel far on the road leaving Accra before the modern, mostly whitewashed cement-block houses change to clusters of small adobe structures with corrugated tin or fiber roofs. Occasionally you pass a hotel or the mansion of a chief or wealthy person who has built in his hometown—the domain of his ancestors and clan;

usually only returning to these homes for obligatory rites, most often funerals. The lack of development is striking on the ninety-eight-mile stretch to Keta, Denu, and then the Aflao border with Togo. Poor roads, collisions, slow-moving, overburdened trucks, and endless customs checkpoints can slow a little over a hundred miles to a half-day's journey. The story of that road is revealing of its precolonial and later colonial makings: from Ivory Coast to Togo, four hundred miles of coastal routes were devised mainly for the extraction of human beings, sumptuary items, and raw materials.

I was becoming more fascinated by the stories of indigo's trade. In the colonial era, most of the indigo that was supplied by Europeans on the West African coast was simple loom-patterned, piece-dyed cloth used for daily wear. (Plain white, undyed cloth was its counterpart.) Known as "Guinea cloth," it was woven in India, shipped to Europe, and then re-exported by slavers to the West Indies and West Africa, before it was eventually industrialized in European factories. Guinea cloth became popular and yielded enormous European profits because it supplemented local weaving, and the cloths were often sold cheaper than those that had to be transported between the coast and the interior.

At the same time European merchants were struggling to compete against aggressive African and Luso-African (a broad term for peoples of various Portuguese and African cultural and racial mixes) cloth traders. These men, almost exclusively, were well-connected, sophisticated businesspeople who made huge profits with their ability to negotiate European and African power, often through familial connections on both sides, their knowledge of the fine differences in what both Europeans and African elites desired in each locale; and their access to the interior trade routes.

These Luso-African merchants worked between the Cape Verde Islands, a remote, archipelago off the coast of Senegal, and ports at the Gabon estuary and in Angola, both in Central Africa, where traders exchanged ivory and slaves for indigo. Portuguese colonialists, the first Europeans to arrive in West Africa, had set up posts in previously uninhabited Cape Verde in the fifteenth century to resupply passing ships, later developing cotton and indigo plantations there. On these plantations, in small workshops under merchant supervision, skilled slaves spun, wove, and dyed some of the most valued and elaborately patterned indigo cloths. African and Luso-African merchants were able to exploit their presence at an early, pivotal period of the Atlantic trade, and so by the seventeenth century their weavers were producing loom-made cloths, dyed indigo or patterned with indigo stripes, that were being exported as far as the West Indies and Brazil.

In the modern era African merchants, big and small, moved indigo and other cloths from Congo, in southern Central Africa, to Senegal, at the continent's westernmost tip. They transported cloth in steamships, in Peugeot six-seaters, on bicycles and motorbikes; they carried it on their heads; they used elaborate networks of agents, porters, and traders based on kinship systems and birthplace. Even the shorter journey from Nigeria to Ghana saw a staggering level of trade. There are records of consignments of cloth—as much as a thousand pounds at a time—being shipped from the interior of Nigeria to Lagos by rail, to Accra by sea, on to Kumasi by rail, and then farther north by road.

Our Peugeot would pass a small town, and then we'd travel for untrafficked miles until we began to see people along the road, carrying goods on their heads. That suggested we were nearing a town or village with a weekly market to which they journeyed. Our driver stopped once, in what appeared to be deep bush, to nervously check his engine; I watched three women appear from a path, walking in stride, carrying on their heads small, precise stacks of wax cloth with the bottom layers curved around their skulls. I recognized that I was in step with history.

We were by then near Klikor-Agbozume, a Ghanaian village near the Togo border. The woman sitting next to me with the dried fish called to the driver. She alighted at the junction to Klikor, and while the driver again worked under the hood, she placed one basket into the other and her patent leather bag atop, lifted them all to her head, and disappeared quickly down a dirt road.

During the ride I had felt disturbed by her but wasn't sure why. She was interesting to puzzle over. Her skin was chalky white with scattered pink abrasions—telltale signs of the use of skin-bleaching cream. She looked like she had been washed in watery white paint or kaolin clay, like a relic of the Ewe shrines, a figure you expected to see tucked in someone's bosom, between layers of carnelian and white and blue beads, during a festival.

Three tiny marks were cut into her face at the center of her eyebrows and on each cheek—typical of Ewe peoples. They were bluish, like a fading tattoo. They also looked like the inverse patterns of an indigo cloth, the marks so blue against her whiteness. I stared at them a little, though I knew it was the result of the creams, which don't fully penetrate scar tissues and often leave bluish-blackish places in the skin. When the woman was younger and brown, she would have been quite beautiful, but this terrible kind of beauty was evidence of a twisted vanity. We talked a little, with a wall of reserve between us that was uncharacteristic of Ghanaians, as if we had some kind of uncomfortable history, but I couldn't imagine what it would be. She revealed she was a trader in Accra and was returning to her hometown for a visit.

I had visited Klikor once with a Ghanaian and Jewish-American friend, Afi, whose father owned a luxury hotel in the region. A few days before we arrived, Afi had found in the morning paper an announcement for the annual festival of the Adzima shrines—the home of the entranced, bare-breasted woman in the blue wrapper I'd witnessed on the road in front of Eurama's shop in those first months. Afi and I had gone to the festival, hoping to get a peek into the world of the *trokosi*, or "wives of the gods."

*Trokosi* (or *fiasidi*, as it is also called) is an ancient Ewe penal system under which crime and punishment are inheritable. With *trokosi*, if someone commits a crime—or if a family carries a social debt or a legacy of monetary debt, in some cases even decades earlier—and particularly if that debt could be attributed to recent misfortune, the family is forced to atone to the gods. The land or other property of the guilty party is impounded, and the virgin daughter or other female kin, usually a child six to ten years old, is sent to the shrine priest to repair the sins of her relative. The girl becomes an initiate of the shrine, the "wife of the gods," and the literal slave of the shrine priest. The Ewe believe that this giving over of a virgin, who is considered pure and closest to embodying human virtue, will restore protection and righteousness to the perpetrator's family. For the girls, it means a life of co-wivery and toil to the priest and shrine community, working nearby plantations and other sometimes-considerable business holdings. The women and girls are uneducated, untrained, and often kept in an altered state with native medicines.

As Afi and I stood barefoot on the edge of the procession, in borrowed wrappers that we were asked to wear before entering the area near to the shrine at the village's center, we had not really understood what we were watching. The men leading the procession through the hard-packed dirt roads in the elaborate hive of adobe structures, carried a large fetish object, the size of a child's body covered in cloth. I imagined that it was a corpse. I'd heard that during the shrine initiations the girls were branded on their faces and bodies, their heads were shaved, and a symbol of their now "deceased" body was dismembered, the parts bound together and dragged around, then put on rack in the shrine to become permanent relics of the gods. The *trokosi* are now under the watch of a local human rights movement involving world agencies like the UN and large NGOs who call for its abolition and the rehabilitation of the 35,000 to 40,000 girls and women, many of whom represent generations of indenturehood.

Many of the women were dressed in blue wrappers, tied at the breasts and waist, with the white and blue and carnelian-colored beads at their upper arms and calves, and white kaolin clay markings on their faces and legs and arms and chests. Other women appeared, dressed similarly, but in varied blue wax prints and calicoes. It was a self-conscious festival-making. Women also sat in a group near the shrine, most of them in simple blue cotton cloths like factory-made Guinea cloths, or yellow and blue cloths—the shrine colors—with a look of poverty in their bodies. We'd approached them to ask where we could buy food, a cold drink, but we barely got replies.

Afterward we visited a strange "center for research" in town, a small chamber with a few unremarkable items on display and odd, jumbled pamphlets about Ewe culture and history for sale. The man who ran it was the person who had approached us soon after we arrived in the village, insisting that we change into cloth. I asked him about indigo and why so many women wore blue. In reply, as we left he handed me a page of frenzied writing with a meandering argument in favor of *trokosi* and why it was misunderstood. At the bottom he'd written, "Indigo is the color of the snake god ancestral shrines, the hunter god, and the thunder god." There would be no answers today.

The visit had felt like my encounter with this woman beside me in the Peugeot—solicitous but defensive, cloaked in wariness and secrecy, if not simple inscrutability. Something about her manner suggested that there might be some connection between us, some reason for reserve. Many months later, when I looked at the photos I'd taken at the festival, this woman appeared in some of them, dressed in blue cloth, with a matching blue tied on her head. Long yellow beads and carnelian adorned her upper arms, and a wax cloth was tied at her waist with a yellow cell phone design. She was sitting with other women near the shrine. In the eye of the camera she has the pallor of a corpse lit by the bright blue marks on her face, and she is oddly smiling.

A short distance beyond Klikor the road widens, the heavy bush giving way to hard-packed, bare earth filled with a clatter of structures. You pass three or four checkpoints along the road, and then amid a frenzy of vehicles and bodies, you are at the Ghana-Togo border—a simple walk across a fifty-yard-long aisle, much like a passage at a bus terminal, herded by customs officers with sticks. I came to love the borders the way I loved the marketplace: the push and pull of bodies, the strong smells, the filth, the jokes and friendships, the brutal underside of exchange, the turbulence and tensions that accrue when so much is at stake. Amid fears of inquiry, bribe-taking, taxing, and the contesting of identities, the borders are where Africans meet in the frenzy of commerce. Money-changers, border guards, customs officers, traders, and hustlers rule the frontier. People clutch their U.S., Russian, Congo, Chad, or Egyptian passports; the market women do their weekly provisions run from Abidjan; the pineapple trader worries about what the heat and the delay are doing to his goods, so loaded with natural sugar that they will easily spoil on the road. All around you much is being bought and sold—the illicit, the exotic, and quotidian. I am fixated on the display of cloth—the swirling mass of bodies cloaked in myriad ways. As citizens of all of Africa pass to and fro in a narrow corral of gates, I watch for indigo treasures.

After a short ride between the border and Lomé, the capital of Togo, on a hired Mobylette, a moped, I'm standing in the Central Market. The market is like many in Ghana, and you can see the two countries' reliance on each other, exchanging goods through years of Ghana's recession and Togo's political upheavals. But floating above the crowds on shiny head trays are fresh loaves of French bread, imported strawberries and green apples, and sweet, dark magenta *bissap* juice, made from hibiscus flowers, in tiny plastic sachets. They signal a kind of decadence that you see only in the former French West African colonies. There are endless stalls filled with soaps and washing powders, toothpastes, deodorants, margarines, and cooking oils—most Lever Brothers brands. The ascendancy of Coca-Cola and Lever Brothers is touted from umbrellas to get customers out of the sun and shiny new refrigerators bearing the company names.

In the 1930s the United Africa Company (UAC), a British entity that was by this time the dominant trading house in West Africa, came under the control of Unilever, the parent of Lever Brothers. The company's profits were built on the principles and practices of the earlier trade in slaves and cloth and raw materials, and it continued to extract raw materials such as palm oil and palm kernels, in turn dominating Africa's import market by making soap and margarine from them and selling them back to African nations at high profit margins. By the time Ghana achieved independence in 1957, UAC was the largest importer of printed cloth from Dutch factories, which were one quarter of exports from the Netherlands to West Africa, and Vlisco dominated.

Kwame Nkrumah, Ghana's first prime minister and then its president, and a founding member of the Organization of African Unity, was cognizant when he took power of the need to balance the scales between Ghana and the former colonial rulers. He soon doubled the import tax on cloth and tried to create incentives for local production, hoping to end the country's dependency on foreign manufacturing. Countries like Nigeria, which gained independence in 1960, soon followed Nkrumah's lead. Vlisco was able to craftily work its way around the taxes, extending special credit arrangements to the cloth sellers in Togo, and openly encouraging smuggling across the Ghana and Benin and Nigerian borders. As much as tastes for Vlisco were born in Ghana, it is Togo's market women who, in many ways, built a stronghold for the company. I wanted to see the fabled Mama Benz, the Togo cloth sellers, whose wealth and power was said to "pass the African Big Men's." Surely, women in the Francophone West African countries were showier, more extravagant in their tastes than in places like Ghana, were one's money was often hidden away or displayed more subtly; where the most marked evidence of it was in the number of extended family members and other persons it was apparent someone was supporting. Already, I could see a difference in the predominance of expensive neon-colored wax cloths, in contrast to Ghana's darker, earthen tones. These were mixed with even costlier lace trims and wrappers and scarves. These were the "daughters" of the Mama Benz, ordinary women, struggling in the heat and dust of the noonday sun.

In Accra the large cloth stores dotting the main thoroughfares of Makola are run by market queens. Women like Eurama's friend, Aunty Araba, own them; she returned from working as a nurses' aide in Maryland to build an empire, first selling Igloo ice coolers to funeral-goers carrying private feasts and smaller traders for whom the electricity to refrigerate the drinks and foods they sold was unreliable. A very dark woman, full of spunk, with the intense, wide-set large eyes, a full mouth, black skin, and a thick, shapely body that is the Akan ideal, she favored *kabas* sewn in the latest Vlisco and drove a shiny new Ford pickup—a rarity in Accra. Aunty Mercy was the only other woman I'd seen drive one. Aunty Araba was the *magadjer*, the high priestess of the streets.

Lomé "store women" strictly drive Mercedes. You can see their sedans parked on the market streets, often covered in a tarpaulin, the driver standing watch with a chamois cloth in his hand. In their shops, they sit high behind the counter, large bodied, breasts heaved up on a stack of cloth, bedecked in gold, sporting gold-rimmed spectacles; from a distance their faces look like whorls in the grand flowering of their elaborate dress fronts and sleeves. They commandeer an army of smaller traders who are at the mercy of an extensive system of credit to both individual buyers and other traders. Their shops are lively with a flow of women competing for exclusive picks on new designs and colors.

The Mama Benz rose out of these throngs. Most of these women are illiterate and have little or no formal education or training. But they were the women who were able to negotiate, to find their way in and to build capital, slowly enlarging their shares of exclusive stock—especially Vlisco cloths—that they in turn sell in smaller pieces, pocketing big profits. Historically, many had liaisons with Dutchmen, sexual or otherwise, a practice encouraged by the heads of Vlisco, who have cynically exploited Togo and Ghana's uneasy trade relationship, giving special privileges to Mama Benz. Vlisco also decided to market almost exclusively to women buyers and at the same time exploit local systems of patronage and a culture of nepotism. By choosing individual women as agents, often offering simple cloth in exchange for knowledge and market information, both Vlisco and the Mama Benz reign.

Among the hundred and fifty new cloth designs that Vlisco introduces each year, one is usually a tribute to the

Mama Benz, refashioned from iconic Vlisco designs. The 2010 cloth is almost kitschy, featuring a flowery field, with "Mama" written in boldface below the iconic emblem of the Benz. The designers in Helmond, sitting at their computers and imagining African women's tastes, know that each cloth is either approved or pronounced dead on arrival in the Mama Benz shops. Mama Benz have become the agents of the wit and creativity of the women who buy from them and the culture of the marketplace, all of which have their roots in the aesthetic of African and Asian ancient indigo cloths. The staple cloth designs, the ones that have so endured that they are given names and assigned proverbs and meanings, have remained in circulation now for decades, some nearly a century and a half. The Mama Benz write these cloths in or out of history with a quick, discerning glance.

I didn't expect to find any hand-dyed indigo in the market, but there were indeed a few cloths, dyed with a synthetic agent on cheap calico, poorer cousins of the icons worn in the Penn photographs. I bought four of them from a woman selling at a tiny freestanding kiosk in the shadow of a large store. That was my own tribute to the woman's strivings and my own, and to indigo's ghost, on the palms of the Mama Benz, and in the air around us, phantom particles floating in the blazing sun, settling on the fridges and margarine tins and soap powder boxes in the market, items sent south by Unilever as new day wares for homemaking. Indigo profits that built the Vlisco empire.

*　　*　　*

So powerful was Irving Penn's remaking of the myth of the Mino, or Amazons, that fifteen years after I'd seen the photographs, and even while the images trouble me, I walked the streets of Abomey, the former capital of the ancient Dahomey empire, still expecting to meet these girls, stubbornly resisting the idea that they had never existed as he had seen them through the camera's eye.

*Amazon* is a European name, inspired by the women of Greek myth, that was bestowed on the royal body-guards and shock troopers of Dahomey, a kingdom whose power and influence was as great as that of ancient Rome's. The Mino were established under King Houegbadja (ruled 1645–85) and were later developed by his son King Agadja (ruled 1708–32) into a militia of four thousand "black virgins," who fought until the late nineteenth century. As the colonial record portrays, they were trained for and married to "the husband that clothes and feeds us": war. They were renowned for their fierce-ness and discipline in battle, for their fearlessness and thirst for bloodletting. They are said to have performed brutal decapitations and to have used Danish guns obtained in exchange for slaves. Because of their power, and because their initiations and war making were closely tied to Vodun, a traditional religion indigenous to Dahomey, they were given a semi-sacred status.

I looked for the Mino and their indigo legacy around me, but in truth Abomey felt like a town of ghosts. I was struck by the poverty; falling-down, tiny, unadorned modern block buildings filled the streets. When I reached the junction where the remains of the Amazon quarters were said to be, I found only the sunken frames of later-built houses.

Women whizzed by on Mobylettes and scooters in a blur of the neon brights of Vlisco's high-end Super Wax cloth, marketed especially to Benin and Ivory Coast. Every young woman, it seemed, had shaved her eyebrows and penciled in new ones with electric blue, fluorescent orange, or red—a newfangled expression of adornment once made with indigo. They seemed to live in a specter of a kind of hyper-modernity, flying across a decaying city built on ancient killing grounds.

I reached the site of the royal palaces, the centuries-old seat of the government of the Kingdom of Dahomey that are now a UNESCO World Heritage Site. With their spectacular architecture and the rich spoils of conquest housed in their halls and temples and tombs, I felt a glimmer of hope for some relic of that blue past. I joined a tour and walked through the many chambers and anterior structures, stunned by the beauty, and how complete and well preserved the historical record was in this region where everything of value as art or social document is extracted by the West or exchanged. But I was disappointed not to see any indigo.

When the tour ended, I asked the guide about indigo, hoping there was something overlooked. He pulled me back along the corridors to the magnificent bas-reliefs, recast and preserved on the palace walls. They chronicle in signs and symbols and figures the ancient state record—predating colonial texts—of the reign of the twelve Fon kings of Dahomey, from 1600 to 1900. The

Mino appear as small figures, with weapons, bare breasts, and blue wrappers, but they are simply a footnote to the kings' record-making, powerful backup girls. The colors used in the bas-reliefs are soul-catching red and blue and yellow and green, in milky and mattelike hues. The guide explained to me that underneath these vivid colors are deeper layers of pigments made from dried and ground indigo leaves, as well as wild gingerroot, kaolin, wood powder, and lamp soot, used to color the hard earth taken from termite mounds.

Inscribed in the walls is the legend of Dako Danzo, also known as Dakodonou, who reigned from 1620 to 1645 as the Kingdom's second monarch. Dako stands out as a man of exceptional cruelty in three centuries of absolute monarchy, a system rare in precolonial Africa and the last to fall to European colonization.

"This is Dako's emblem," the guide said. "You see what I am pointing to? This is a tinderbox. This is a war club. This is indigo."

Indigo was a simple image of a pot, with blue spheres inside, floating among the other images on the wall.

Dako is said to have killed a farmer or indigo planter, Donou, in a pot of indigo, and to have made sport of the killing, rolling the corpse around in its fetid blue tomb. "Dako kills Donou as easily as breaking an indigo jar" is the motto preserved by history.

"The farmer's name, Donou, was taken by Dako: Dakodonou. This death gave origin to the name Dahomey," said the guide.

He could not explain much more, and though I've

tried to uncover what the farmer's death symbolized, and what the insult or deathly power of the indigo vat actually meant in that age, the story seems lost to history. Some records say that Dako killed his mother-in-law by the same means. All we can rely on is the image on the walls.

The guide pointed me to the old quarter of town as a place to search for indigo cloths, and indeed, I soon spied, over the lip of an earthen wall, a calabash, or dried gourd bowl, and a gathering of small blue fibrous balls—pounded and rolled indigo leaves spread out to dry in the sun. A goat kept passing over them, scattering them more widely on the ground. Against the wall of a small house were four clay dye pots covered with rubber pans, and hanging on a stack of cement blocks were three blue-black cloths, puckered at one hem from the stitched patterning that would be untied to reveal a design of white resist to the dye.

Inside the house I found an old woman and several very small children. None of them spoke English or French, but we signed until we had some understanding. Madame Honegbeto, the old lady, showed me the cloths that were drying; simple, lovely patterns on thin calico like the ones I'd purchased in Lomé. She took a stick and began to stir one of the dye pots. I thought for a while about staying on there and trying to learn more, but a funny pull in me said I should leave, taking only what I'd seen. I can't explain it really, except that it felt like the contentment of arriving at something after long ardor, then looking in, but not wanting to linger. It was as if staying would require more of both of us than I wanted.

I stooped to look at the indigo balls, small and whorly and dense but light as paper. Their sweet, acrid smell had become as familiar as the smell of cedar in my grandmother's drawers. The old lady gave me some of them, wrapped in a small scrap of a cloth. It was a generous gift; the balls were costly. They filled my head with the pleasure I'd come to know, and all the way home to Accra, I would keep them in my bag and sniff at them. But before I reached home, they grew moldy, and when Eurama spotted insects in them, she swept them into the gutter without a glance. A photo I took in the old woman's yard shows traces of them. The balls are strewn about, a goat is disappearing from the frame, and the surroundings look desolate and gray, as if they are relics from a world long past.

Walking farther into the center of Abomey, I spied the daughters of the Amazons everywhere, in polyester dresses from China, blue jeans, and couture-tailored Vlisco. Indigo cloth was easy to find, in the same patterns that the girls wear in the Penn photos. I'd discovered that those designs are quotidian, made with a few balls of indigo thrown into synthetic dye. They are sold almost everywhere in Abomey—in tourist shops, by the roadside, in cafés—where you can also find cheap copies of the colorful Fon appliqués, much celebrated by collectors, fashioned after the bas-reliefs, adorned with signs and figures and, almost always, a tiny indigo pot.

I decided then to travel southwest from Abomey,

hoping to reach Porto Novo before nightfall. In the late afternoon I arrived in the Yoruba city. The dress and language were Yoruba; the people had a posture, a different way of being, a distinct fire in the belly, that was familiar to me. I thought about going on and crossing into Nigeria. I was so close now to Lagos, the gateway to the blue lands of southwestern Nigeria. I could sleep in Porto Novo and arrive in Ibadan, the professor's hometown, before nightfall the next day. But I decided instead on a slow return west. The borders between Benin and Togo and Ghana were calling out to me again.

# SEVEN

# Not Everything You Can Own, Ivory Coast

Koua Aya's compound was cool. The light filtered into her workroom and illuminated the bent, shaven heads of the old women working beside her. Pots, some as high as my thigh, were still slick with water, the light yellow-brown color of an infant's stool. Others were fired a deep glinty brown. Delicate birds alighted on a vase, a ram's head morphed into a woman's thighs, and small, stud-like designs circled the rim of a plate, all splendid, other-wordly forms.

Koua Aya was tiny and lithe. Her head too was shorn, the sign that she was past menopause, and had reached the age and stature of a master of fecundity and earth. She was laughing when I arrived and told her I'd come to Tanoh Sakassou by road from Accra, a twenty-two-hour trip, in search of her studio. Long ago I'd bought a vase from her workshop in a New York museum and put the tag that accompanied it in my notebook, hoping I might one day visit her compound, not thinking then that she might be my gateway to indigo dyers. Where there is indigo dyeing, someone suggested to me, there are pots. It was a revelation for my attempt not to floun-der and squander my time as I set out for the land of the Baule.

"There is no petrol in Côte d'Ivoire, and you are here?" she teased. Our driver stood anxiously near the road. I'd hired a car in Bouaké and set off to the village without much of an address, trusting to wit. The driver had warned that we'd need to return before dusk; we must not tarry on the road or burn through our less-than-full tank. I picked frantically among the pots, possessed by a mounting anxiety. It was not the fuel crisis; in Ghana and Togo and Benin and Mali there had always been someone at the roadside offering a jerry can or siphon for the right price, so I assumed I could buy contraband petrol. No, I was afraid that this world I'd just alighted in, beauty and spirit-filled, would slip away without my being able to enter it at all. I might return the next day, but when the journey there took so long, each hour was precious, and something in the air told me that another trip might be impossible. I picked out more pots than I could carry back to Accra and then to New York, surprised and embarrassed at this new urge to hoard.

As the shop boys pulled newspaper from a storage shelf, I spied on the shelf the dark blue rough hide of something rolled.

"Oh, is that indigo?" I asked. They pulled it down and unfurled three yards of cloth made from bark fibers—tightly amassed, soft, rootlike threads that had been dyed and then pounded or rubbed with indigo powder. It was stunning. Bark cloth is most commonly associated with Uganda, where the art has a recognized history of more than six hundred years. I had not considered it at all part of an indigo legacy. I asked Koua Aya about it, and she explained that the art was a tradition of the Beng people; someone had commissioned the cloth and would use it as a ceremonial mat or for ceremonial attire. She described the process of cutting down a tree, stripping the trunk, making a pulp, forming and drying it, then sending it to a local dyer.

"We hide these things. To make it, you have to take down a whole tree, and it is illegal," one of the boys explained. "So the police raid the places where it is sold."

I asked them if I could buy it, hearing Eurama hiss in my ear, "*Not everything you can own, my dear Catherine. The beautiful ones are not for any one of us, really.*"

Koua Aya laughed and shook her head. "It belongs to someone," she said. But she handed a knife to one of the boys and instructed him to cut a small piece from the edge for me, and they tucked it in between the pots. She promised to tell me more about it, and send me to the dyers, when I returned in the morning.

The driver was hovering now at the door, and his fidgeting presence unsettled me. We said good-bye, and during the car ride to Bouaké, I smelled and fingered the patch of cloth like a flower, worried about the road ahead.

In Bouaké, a sure tension hovered over everything. There was talk of a worsening gas strike, of a bus strike scheduled for the next day. Rumor had it that the gas shortage had been orchestrated and was the advent of a police and military strike.

I was traveling with Eurama's son, Kwesi, on his first trip outside Ghana. He had just finished college and was going to be starting a job at a bank in Accra. He wanted to see fabled Abidjan, spoken of as Africa's Paris, the capital of Ivory Coast. We had gone there first. As we traveled, I explained that he was "my husband's small brother" to signal that I was not a tourist and he was not my silly boyfriend, because relationships—probably more than anything—define every West African encounter. But despite our story-making, everyone had assumed that Kwesi, with his neat khakis, polo shirts, and Anglophone cosmopolitan swagger, was South African. Customs officers, hoping he had South African rands, had harassed us at endless checkpoints ever since we crossed the border from Ghana into Ivory Coast.

It was hard to understand what was happening; no one would speak to us in English and ignored our broken French (a particular Ivorian conceit toward Anglophones), and so Kwesi and I looked for Ghanaians at the taxi terminal and in the market, hoping to find someone who would tell us clearer news and change our *cedis* to CFA francs. We wandered for a long time, searching among the money-changers and the mechanics, until we found a tailor's shop blaring Ghanaian gospel music. The tailor warned us that something big was brewing and advised us to go back to Abidjan.

We spent the night in Bouaké, and the tensions around us seemed to intensify in the night traffic. We tossed and turned to the sounds from the street below. I slowly let go of the chance of meeting Koua Aya again and in the early morning we boarded a bus for Abidjan, surprised that I did not feel my usual stubbornness about staying on. Six months earlier there had been a coup in Ivory Coast, and I had taken others' advice and waited it out, listening to the news for assurance that the situation had become more stable. By the time I planned the trip, these same people advised, "It could be your last good chance for a while."

At the bus terminal there was a boutique selling Baule indigo wrappers, cheap copies of the cloth I'd chased in Bobo-Dioulasso, woven from machine-manufactured threads. I'd seen many weavers on the road from Abidjan, their ground looms stationed along the highway, their cloths hung for sale from trees and on racks. In the flash of an eye from a moving car they were quite lovely, but they had not even been facsimiles of the complex old Baule mastery. I searched through similar cloths at the boutique, admiring the work. I purchased two wrappers and a heavy woven man's cloth that was thoroughly modern, royal blue with fluorescent pink and green and yellow details. I was beginning to appreciate that in West Africa new is not a devaluing measure. Innovation is king, right alongside tradition. I marveled at this fact as much as at the bark cloth.

I was sad to be leaving at a moment of so much discovery. We'll go back to Abidjan and see how things settle, I told Kwesi. Something told me we wouldn't return.

\*     \*     \*

The morning after we arrived in Abidjan, Kwesi and I rose early and set out to explore the city. The tensions of Bouaké had only increased there, and it became hard to hide our discomfort as we waited too long for a bus that would take us into the city's commercial center. At first we blamed the delay on the surprisingly cool, soaking rain. We eventually saw a taxi and flagged it down. It took us to the main thoroughfare; we alighted at a junction where it should have been easy to get further transportation. The junction was crowded with pedestrians, but there were no cars on the road. We waited more than twenty minutes without seeing any vehicles, and then slowly, one by one, cars and buses began to round the bend. Then traffic seemed to slowly increase. But nearly every vehicle had a soldier at the wheel, and those cars began to race against the few driven by private citizens, heading them off, pulling the passengers out, and leaving them standing in the road.

We soon heard shots, and the crowd farther down from us convulsed with panic, which lit the people around us like a wildfire. Kwesi and I ran with them back down the road leading away from the city center. By now the rain was falling hard. Several miles up the sloping highway, everyone was walking in the rain. Shots still rang in the air. In our line of grim travelers, no one was talking, and no one would respond to our questions. For nearly a mile, no cars passed us—then the sound of a motor would cut the air, and everyone would grow tenser, then breathe relief as the soldiers passed without incident.

More than an hour later we arrived at our hotel to eerie quiet. We sat at the bar and watched the minister of communications—a dark, hedged soul, his words barely enunciated—explain that the soldiers were on strike because they'd received no pay since the coup that had brought Robert Guéï to power less than a year before. As a result the borders, the airports, the banks, the TV and radio stations, and all businesses in the city were closed. Kwesi and I looked at each other, unable to talk, as this dramatic news surrendered to a video of an Ivorian band doing a cover of a D'Angelo song. Hotel guests, who had appeared at the first sound of official news reporting, milled about, impeccably dressed, in the suits and jewels and fancy coiffures that Ivorians favor as day wear.

Kwesi and I waited there for more than an hour, hoping to hear something more, then retreated to our rooms to rest. We were worried, but that refuge seemed the only way to fight the anxious pull at our bodies.

I tried to read but kept obsessing about what I'd left behind in Bouaké. I had little chance of returning there now, I knew. This was my fifth trip to Ivory Coast, the others while I was on extended layovers on flights between Ghana and other West African destinations. I would have another opportunity to visit Koua Aya, I reasoned. I didn't know that Bouaké was about to become a frontier in a civil war.

In the late afternoon, after we had spent hours in the dark suite under the unnerving hum of the air conditioning, the sounds of shelling seemed to stop. I called Kwesi, and we rejoined the crowd at the bar who watched the same Ivorian band doing R&B music covers. We decided to venture outside.

We sat for a long time by the roadside near the hotel, scared to go far. As the sun descended and the mosquitoes began their wild reign, the hotel staff huddled in small groups near the back gate, talking, and I approached them to see what they could tell me of the situation. No one had news, but they were anxious to get home before dark. The thought of their leaving made the hotel suddenly seem open and vulnerable, its garden refuge no longer desirable. I felt truly panicked, but everyone else, even Kwesi, showed a studied calm, and I tried to master my countenance.

For almost an hour we turned the possibilities over in our heads, but then the sound of shots broke in the air. Vehicles again flew along the open road, an army man at every wheel, rifle butts stuck out of the car windows. One car slowed down and turned onto the road toward the hotel. A man wearing a gas mask gave us his slow regard. Another small truck followed, a bazooka rifle sticking high out of the back window. Kwesi and I looked at each other. Should we return to our room or head for another part of town? We sat frozen by the road, wanting to appear unbothered, until a man we recognized from the hotel passed hurriedly in his uniform.

"Are things okay inside?" I asked. "Is it safe?"

"Cool," he replied in studied French. "They dropped some men off at the bar and moved on."

We went back to our room and hurriedly packed

our things, anticipating that we would need to leave, and then we went to the bar and ordered a meal. As we dined, I thought about my folly. How was I to carry this heavy load of cloth and pottery? What was my stubborn need to have it all and to take it all with me? The army men, sitting drinking, seemed somehow innocuous, as if this were an everyday affair, despite the sound of shelling in the distance and their weapons parked against their chairs. An Ivorian woman sat at the next table in a French-cut skirt suit with a Chanel bag beside her, eating in silence with her companion. She patiently ate her rice from the blade of a knife; the staff had mostly left and the bartender was making do, with no time to wash dishes. Kwesi and I looked at each other with the same thought: There was something wrong with Ivory Coast, with all its Parisian pretensions. If this were Ghana, she would eat with her hands. And still be a lady. Afterward we laughed about it, but in the back of my mind I thought, *I'm just like her; I'm unable to give up the ghost of the things I hope will fill me with meaning.*

The television whirred; then the screen came to life. An army man announced that there was widespread looting in the city, and several banks had been robbed that morning. A curfew had been imposed; everyone was required to be indoors by nightfall.

At seven o'clock they broadcast a presidential address. President Guéï said the forces in the street were members of a breakaway army. The government would settle with the army; negotiations were under way. In the meanwhile the status quo would continue: the borders, banks, airport, and news channels would remain closed until further notice.

As the hours passed, the bar filled with more men in military uniforms.

Back in our rooms I packed and unpacked, so that I had different combinations of what to leave behind and what to bring along. I settled on bringing the cloth and three of Koua Aya's pots; I unloaded most of my clothing and books. But still my bag was heavy and cumbersome, and I felt ashamed of my desire for these things.

That night we slept uneasily, with Guéï's words in our heads.

Early the next morning Kwesi and I walked in the already-blazing sunshine away from Les Deux Plateaux, a swank, mostly residential district, toward Le Plateau, the city's center. We saw growing movement in the streets; I wanted to believe the city had restored itself, but the voice of the woman I'd spoken to at the U.S. embassy stayed in my ear: *"The situation is still too fluid. There are too many factions to understand which way things will go. So we advise that you lie low and keep in close contact."*

When we reached the highway, the gleaming tower of the famous Hôtel Ivoire, the tallest point of Le Plateau, loomed before us. I was desperate to be back indoors. What strange figures we cut, the "half-caste" American woman and the younger "South African" man, walking alone on a highway, with travel bags and a cumbersome box, not on their heads, but uncomfortably in their hands.

We worried about each vehicle that passed, with its inevitable uniformed driver. The army men hung cavalierly off trucks and halfway out the doors and windows of buses; they seemed not to notice us, but how easily that might change. Ahead of us on the road others walked with purposeful steps, like a caravan, in a single line along the meridian. It took some time for me to register that everyone was moving in the opposite direction from us. I went in circles in my mind about what to do. Should we continue to the Hôtel Ivoire, a five-star hotel with its own ice rink, restaurants, and shops, where we might get a bank and would be among the expatriate community and other elites who could afford protection? Should we return to Les Deux Plateaux? Or go straight to the embassy? Should we pay money to a man we'd met at the hotel bar who offered to deliver us to a less trafficked northeastern border, where we might bribe our way into Ghana?

Soldiers at the makeshift checkpoints on the road and others passing in cars offered us rides or a resting place, but we moved on, surprised by their gentlemanly posture with the soundtrack of intervals of gunfire. We walked for many miles that day, on to Cocody and then to the near end of Plateau, from the Hôtel Ivoire to the embassy, past groups of French soldiers manning the gates of banks and the shattered windows of the highest-end French designer boutiques—the vestiges of a city with an unusual cosmopolitanism now pitched into chaos and fear. When shots began to ring closer to us, in rapid bursts, we decided on the gleaming tower of the Hôtel Novotel, a low-key, friendly, French-owned refuge with a good pool and good food. I sometimes sought the hotel from the same chain in Accra, when the city dirt and lack of privacy became overwhelming. We arrived dirty, with my worn cardboard box, after nearly fifteen miles of walking, and booked a room amid other worried travelers hunkering down for another night.

The next morning, viewed from the balcony, the city appeared utterly normal. A gas station was servicing cars driven by civilians; traffic flew along the highways; pedestrians walked in their finery, with a different purposefulness, toward offices and the shops.

The official word was that the borders were reopened, though the curfew was still in place. Kwesi and I anxiously dressed and headed for the bus terminal, hoping to make it to Accra by nightfall. We got seats in a Peugeot wagon next to a thin, wizened civil servant from Senegal en route to Benin; a Cameroonian student going home from Conakry, Guinea; and an Ivorian woman whose huge body was made even more voluminous by her boubou and multiple scarves. She talked unceasingly, seeming to take all the air out of the car. Our driver was a mad fellow, abusing us all, talking endlessly about our extra bags, especially my offending box, and promising to collect more money for "overweight" or leave us by the roadside. I calculated in my head: How much would I pay before I would abandon Koua Aya's pots? How much before I let go my cloths? I heard Eurama whispering, *"My dear, please, suppose it is life, a human being, then you hold it like an egg, but not things, things, things."*

Not long out of Abidjan you meet miles and miles of plantations and rice fields; the rich, furiously green land is like no other along the hundreds of miles of coast I'd now traveled between Porto Novo and Abidjan. Everything everywhere else has been extracted and left to spoil, but you escape into this paradise, wanting to forget that it is the domain of French conglomerates and a few elite Ivorians, and that the making of this beauty is the making of the crisis you are escaping.

In the moment of escape I looked inward. With Kwesi, I was lugging these pots and cloths—literal fragments or remakings of a past. Not the thing itself. I faced again the crisis of the collector. What price ownership? Whose heritage was I collecting—my own? That of my ancestors? My ancestor the hero-ine of indigo folklore? I wondered about this intense passion in the midst of a violent, modern remaking of a nation. Koua Aya's pots, the new Baule cloth, and the bark cloth were all so fine but seemed to represent both our quest and our folly: my own and Ivory Coast's. I found myself answering Eurama: *"These things are life."*

Ten miles before the border at Elubo, a tire exploded. We were alone on deserted roads; we had not seen another vehicle for many miles. It was nearly sundown, and the border would soon close. A few days ago Kwesi and I had managed to have a short phone conversation with Eurama by renting someone's cell phone for the call. "Why can't they open the borders for you people, at least? Ask them!" she had demanded. To keep ourselves going for the past few days, Kwesi and I had been laughing about it.

Now Kwesi delivered the punch line to me before I could even joke: "We will! We will ask!"

Our driver had announced he would only go as far as the terminal at the frontier; he would sleep there tonight and return to Abidjan in the morning to make another run. He couldn't have cared less about the border, several miles farther, in a desolate frontier encompassing the separate Ghanaian and Ivorian posts. Now he acted helpless about the tire. Then Kwesi took over and won the argument about our extra load by changing it for him. I was as anxious as the rest, but standing in the thick of the bush, a glorious land bathed in the light of sunset, I pulled the small piece of bark cloth from my bag, held it to the sun, and saw the depth of a blue morass. It seemed a comment on the futility of our quests, on human nothingness.

Our driver dropped us off without ceremony where he promised. We quickly hired a car to take us to the Ghana posts, which a man announced would close in less than a half hour. Before us at the Ghana customs station was a long line of women in blue-black funeral cloth, Ghana's very singular weekend ubiquity, that appeared like a refuge.

"What kind of girl is this? Hei! Shopping through military action? You are completely mad!" Eurama said, pinching my arm sharply as I hung my new cloths on her clothesline to air out in the sunshine.

In Accra we learned that the crisis in Ivory Coast had been an attempted coup. It was the precursor to the civil war that would wrack the country for the next decade. I often thought of Koua Aya, her studio now at a rebel front line.

# The Beautiful One, Ghana

I woke at five A.M. in my room in Osu to the sound of exhortations, so loud they rattled the shutters on Sister's beauty shop, which was too closely butted against my room. If I hadn't heard "Jesu Christo" in every refrain, I would have mistaken the noise for a drunken rant. I put on a dress and went to the veranda, half-expecting that Eurama had sent her church sisters to save me from myself. It was the third week of area funerals. First a twenty-two-year-old boy who became a father post-death. His family said he had died of food poisoning, but the rumors swirled: Maybe his friends had killed him? Was it envy? He would have been leaving for the United States a month later. No one missed the poetry of his being buried in the suit he bought to travel in. Then came the news that a mother and her two children had eaten a dinner of tainted tinned corned beef and were discovered dead in their room the next morning.

Now my landlord's family was preparing to bring another tenant, Alhaji's, body to our yard.

A few weeks before, I had come home at nightfall and walked across the courtyard and past Alhaji's room, aware of an absence. His wife was usually sitting on a stool outside, bare-breasted, shelling beans. She was a bean seller; making lunches of palm oil and beans and plantain. But she was not there that evening. She and Alhaji had quarreled loudly the night before, and that morning she'd packed off noisily.

His door was propped open and the curtain that hung in the doorway was blowing so that as I passed, I could see his feet. He was at his usual post, sitting in his chair under the whirr of the TV. The insects had begun their flights, drawn to the glow of fluorescent light—I wondered why he hadn't shut the screen door. Later that evening a visitor came to the gate and asked the kids playing in the yard to fetch Alhaji. They called to him again and again but couldn't wake him, still sitting in his chair.

Alhaji had pierced his foot at a construction site. He had hobbled around the compound on a foot stained with gentian violet for several days. He was not a drinker, but when I last saw him waving and shouting odd garbled curses at a wandering goat, I assumed he was inebriated. In fact, he'd been dying slowly of tetanus.

The exhorters—my landlord's wife and her church sisters—were there for his wife. His wife was neither Christian or Muslim; she was an Ewe woman from far away, a "stranger" whose family no one knew. She was a "bush girl" who had the bad taste to sit naked in a Christian house. She had left Alhaji in an hour of need. And tetanus? This kind of death was not common and was surely witchcraft.

I dressed and went outside to the veranda to watch the scene but just as soon, Lady Diana appeared at the gate, beckoning to me.

"Maa Eurama said you should come."

\*       \*       \*

Eurama greeted me with a story: Aunty Mercy had pulled up at the shop in her pickup truck the evening before, wearing only a brassiere and a wrapper, her wig tilted on her head, her gold sunglasses askew. She had handed Eurama a head wrap of fine woven Yoruba *asa oke* in three shades of indigo, with a prized magenta raw silk *ikat* running through it.

"Give this to Catherine and tell her she owes me. Oh, never mind, I'll take it in buttons and thread, and she can pay you." Aunty Mercy had then stuffed a large plastic bag with what she needed, a can of sardines and a Guinness from the fridge. Eurama had held her tongue.

Now she held the *asa oke* out to me between two fingertips, her face curled up. "It's fine-o, but see how it is smelling! She took the thing right off her own head, I'm sure. See how she came dressed like she's from her bed, only to steal from me! You cannot pay her for this dirty thing. I'm going to collect my debt, *kra!*" She chuckled. "Anyway, this is not why I called you. Someone is inside. I've given them their breakfast, and they are waiting for you."

In the yard I saw the little girl who lived down the road. Kwale was four years old, slim, the color of dark butterscotch, with a broad face and a high, square fore-head—classic Ga beauty marks. Each morning she walked gracefully along the gutter in only a pair of worn panties, presenting coins for tiny sachets of milk powder, sugar for a family member's tea, or for a sliver of soap. Her reddish hair was thinning and patchy, the telltale signs of kwashiorkor, a disease caused by acute protein deficiency.

Kwale looked like an angel, but she would smile and then insult you. "You, your mouth is sharp like a Makola woman's," Eurama would tell her. One day as Kwale walked away, mumbling about how we resembled monkeys, I called her back and offered her a hard-boiled egg. She ate it hungrily.

"You see! The girls needs protein. And a vitamin shot," Eurama said. "But her mother has at least seven kids, and I don't think she can care for any of them."

Every morning Kwale came, the panties eventually exchanged for a small, worn dress. Sometimes she brought her friend Mamounia, her age-mate, who roamed the area and sold charcoal from a head pan while her mother tended a stall at the junction. I fed them from the shop, and they smiled at me, then ran away laughing, passing insults between them.

"This girl came here this morning crying. She said she is hungry, and when she asked her mother for food, she told her 'Go and see your *obruni*. she is feeding you. Let her be your mother!'

"So take this your cloth. I told you proper indigo will come to you. You know it is a custom to get a blue cloth when you get a baby. They are both dirty things, you see, but they are what your spirit is telling you that you need. You want beautiful things, but beauty comes from caring. So get ready! Go and wash them both. You are a mother now. This child is going to sleep in this house from now on. She's your darling; everyone knows you care for her.

I'll feed her and you can find a school for her and manage her school fees. Even when you leave finally for New York, you can send twenty dollars every month.

"We are burying our Alhaji, too, today. One comes, one goes. It's life-o! Life. Isn't life what you are searching for?"

# nine

# Mothers of Ash, Nigeria

Àdùnní's house in Oshogbo is alive with works of the seen and unseen. It is a Yoruba house. Inspired by the distinctive two-story, boxy, stucco-faced style of the Amaros—men and women who had been enslaved in Brazil but returned to Nigeria seeking a Yoruba motherland beginning in the 1830s. It rises far above the close-knit, single-story houses that surround it. The gates and facade are adorned with elaborate figures and Yoruba spiritual iconographies fashioned from concrete, mixed with ritually prescribed amounts of red earth from the sacred groves of Osun, the goddess of intimacy, beauty, wealth, and diplomacy. They are overrun with bougain-villaea. Goats laze on the long stairs.

A woman meets me on the front steps in a wrapper and blouse, made of indigo *adire* cloth like the professor's, a purple-blue *gele* tied at her head. She is the hard-faced gatekeeper, one of Àdùnní's many adopted children. I tell her about my search and that I've come to greet Mama, the master artist, the great *Iyalaro*, the Mother of Indigo, literally the Mother of Ash, the agent of wizardry in the dyer's pot.

She listens to me with an air of boredom. I am one of many, and a latecomer. Long ago many others came to her, in search mostly of the refuge she had created of the sacred groves of Osun-Oshogbo. Some were worshippers of Osun, hailing from Brazil and Cuba, the United States, Europe—wherever Yoruba and Yoruba-derived religions lived. Many were students and acolytes of the legendary New Sacred Art movement. In the 1960s Àdùnní had helped spawn the Oshogbo School of Art, a community that radically reshaped aesthetics and understandings of African art in Africa and in the West.

The woman ushered me into the house. Its inner shell conjured Russian Art Nouveau, with its decadent, undulating banisters, its wide stairs, the clean lines of the arches high above, pale walls, and high ceilings. In the rooms upstairs, we walked through a wonderful labyrinth of metal and wooden and stone forms—furniture, carved doorways, posts and sculptures, lacelike metal curtains, pots for offerings, plants—all illuminated by bright bursts of sunshine and patches of soft filtering light. It was an Austrian-Yoruba world of the pantheon of Yoruba gods and goddesses. Bright plastic prayer mats, a kettle for ablutions, and a few household items were scattered here and there. I was left in an anteroom, overcome by the feeling of the place that despite its art felt strangely, obversely stark, spare, and intensely calming. I waited for nearly an hour, lulled into dreams by the room's meditative quiet. Then the woman reappeared and told me she'd bring me to Mama, but that I could stay only to greet her.

Àdùnní was frail, bent over with age, her body lost in the voluminous folds of a brilliant but worn green and magenta *agbada*, a men's robe. Her wide-brimmed hat called to mind a Hasidic man's, her face pinched and sunken under it. She looked unflinchingly at me from heavily kohl-lined eyes whose retinas were pushed out, dangling like refulgent blue-gray scales. My shock at her condition immobilized me, left me feeling intrusive and uncomfortable that I had come only to witness, to peer in. I mumbled something about admiration for her and about indigo, and I was invited to snap a photo of her like a tourist. Then the younger woman led me away, asking if I would leave something for Mama. "You see she is very old now, and she needs our care."

Àdùnní was born Susanne Wenger in Austria and had been a resister of Nazism. She was an unusual, stubborn, and avant-garde thinker and painter, whose surrealist work influenced a generation of postwar artists. She married the world-renowned German scholar and historian Ulli Beier, who was also a doyen of Yoruba sacred arts and African literature and theater. He had just accepted a teaching post at University of Ibadan.

They moved to Nigeria in 1950. In her early days there Wenger was infected with tuberculosis. She sought native healers as part of her rehabilitation, which brought her into contact with an important generation of Yoruba priests. She came to understand her illness as part of her initiation as an *olorisha*, one who is inhabited by an *orisha* (a spirit or deity) and a priestess of Obatala, the powerful god who is the custodian of *ori*, one's soul or destiny.

She went about restoring the ancient shrines in the sacred grove along the Osun River, hoping to preserve traditions and spiritual practices in a region where Christianity had run rampant. Throughout the grove she and other artists, priests, and artisans also built their own expressions of the sacred. Their huge, mystical, breathtaking structures were expressions of the gods and goddesses. The sanctuary they created has become world renowned, a place of spiritual pilgrimage as important as any.

Wenger was both revered and hated for her work. The Osun-Oshogbo Sacred Grove came under fierce attack by traditionalists as well as by African and Western progressives, whose unease with the movement was as fierce as the support by spiritual and cultural adherents. At the same time, powerful interests in fishing, lumber, real estate, and farming forced her to seek protection; on occasion she and the grove were physically attacked.

She was a painter primarily, and she continued to paint in Nigeria, but the Western notion of solitude for the artist was too much in conflict with Yoruba society. Eventually she began to work on cloth so that she could work with others or simply in others' company. So began her initiation into indigo, and indigo deepened her initiation into the world of the *orishas*.

In Yoruba, everything in life has a spiritual significance. Even the most rudimentary work is guided by the realm of the spirits, and so as one works, one pays tribute. The goddess Iya Mapo is the patroness of all exclusive women's work, trades like dyeing, pottery, and soap-making. She is the deity of sex. She guides all things erotic. She guides conception and birth. She guides the tricky realm of the indigo dye pot, and the hands of the women and girls who design cloths, perform the intense preparation for dyeing, and undertake the many steps to a finished cloth. So important is Iya Mapo that on the fourth day of each week, on her *ose*, or day of worship, women bring sacrifices of food to her shrines and spend the day celebrating and worshipping her.

Wenger became known as Àdùnní and began to perform the work of the initiate. She also began painting images on cloth that were as significant as her earlier European works. She wore clothing made from indigo *adire* at a time when *adire* was considered out of fashion, a peasant's cloth. She wore her *buba* (a blouse) without its essential mates of a wrapper and *gele* or head wrap. She often wore men's smocks. She was slight and lanky, her hair was cut short or shorn, and her face had a severity and intensity, so she appeared bizarre, even fearsome, to the people around her.

She, along with Ulli Beier and the Nobel Prize-winning author Wole Soyinka, are credited with the revival of *adire*, which led to a recognition and protection of indigo arts and the resurgence of a lucrative market. In fact, a great convergence of politics and personalities and tastes ushered in a new era of blue. In the 1950s and 1960s, when the three wore *adire* shirts, the stewards at the Mbari Mbayo club in Ibadan, a center of avant-garde theater started by the playwright Duro Lapido, began to imitate them. They were joined by students and Peace Corps workers, African-American intellectuals, artists (including Jacob Lawrence), and travelers. The "Mbari shirt" craze began. Street hawkers followed fashion. In the 1960s, after Nigeria achieved independence, indigo *adire* was then worn increasingly by the country's elite as a sign of both Yoruba ethnicity and Nigerian identity.

The era of the 1960s was a powerful recall of a practice in the 1890s and early 1900s, when elite Yoruba women began to incorporate Yoruba clothes—many of them indigo—with European prints, a signal of a rejection of Christian missionary prescriptions on Yoruba dress and cultural practices.

Yet another blue revival had occurred in the 1970s and 1980s. By this time, the older, finest cloths were beginning to have considerable value to Western collectors.

Later, as I walked in the Osun-Oshogbo sacred grove, entranced by the beauty and the feeling of that place, people appeared suddenly. Some begged, some had small boys playing for money on talking drums, some purported to be custodians, shrine-keepers, or guides.

I had arrived in Lagos a few days before, on a Sunday morning, in the midst of an oil strike. The old 747 had flown from Accra, but the wheel that pushed open the doors would not turn, and we eventually had to exit through a tiny hole in the cockpit, down a wobbly wheeled-in staircase. The morning seemed to have an eerie tameness, but on that day more than three hundred people were slain in the city in retaliation for an earlier slaying in the north. A terrible fight for basic resources, and for dignity, was being played out as Muslim-Christian violence. People were being randomly pulled from cars and hacked. The city stank of fire and dead bodies. The car that my hosts drove was stopped repeatedly by ill-outfitted policemen with hunger in their eyes, and these men with Ph.D.'s spoke obsequiously to them, pleading gently that they too were civil servants and I was a visiting student.

The dislocation in Àdùnní's eyes had reached into me. What was I here for? I was a tourist, as much as I was encountering places and people of great meaning to me. All my encounters were fleeting; they were merely helping me to knit together pieces of experience, knowledge, bits of history.

At the University of Ibadan faculty guesthouse was a lone vendor, a lady who had sat there for decades and who remained even after far fewer people traveled there. She found pieces of cloth one by one, visiting old dyeing compounds and cloth sellers, buying from the cloth boxes of old ladies and families eager for cash a few of the literal fragments of it all.

I arrived at her stand on a good day. She showed me four cloths that were very old, pristine, fine examples of important designs. One was Olokun, representing the goddess of the sea, also known as "Life is sweet," a name spun into "Money comes from the sea and makes life sweet," or "Money comes from overseas." The cloth was patterned with abstract forks and knives, kola nuts, chieftancy leaves, a scorpion, and cranes, hand-drawn in cassava paste with a chicken feather, becoming the crackling soft white lines emerging from the soak of dark indigo.

The second was Eiyepe, "All the birds are here," with

fine, intricate patterning of many birds, a blue-black aviary. "No more velvet" was a dark and thick embellished cloth, textured from stitching, a comment on periodic government bans on imported textiles. And finally Sun bebe, or "Lifting up the beads," had sharp, rhythmic patterning, a nod to the eroticism of waist beads and the beauty of the wearer.

I felt something like a thief, and, in fact, my host, Peju, had looked them over and commented that I was one of the people extracting, for very little money, the last bits of a national treasure. Indeed, by 2010, some of the cloths, bought for less than $30, would value at $1,500, and the trader at the faculty guest house rarely finds a single one.

The evening after my visit to the grove, I sat in the compound of a *babalawo*, watching him read the entrails of a chicken I'd presented for sacrifice. The people around him, and the friend who had accompanied me, clapped and offered excited blessings. I would have success in my work; the road was clear for me; it was good work. But I would always battle loneliness. I was to keep a purple cloth with me always, and a broom, or its fibers. I was to sweep the air of this loneliness and wear a favored perfume. I would have strength for my journey because it was just.

Ten years earlier I had consulted a legendary Yoruba priest who had stayed in Brooklyn for some time. I met with him over that year and wasn't quite sure what I was seeking, but I could never break from my fascination. Still, unlike Àdùnní, I could not enter the realm of the believer. The closest expression of the divine had been in my quiet absorption with indigo.

Àdùnní would die in 2009, at the age of ninety-three, eight years after my visit. In 2005 the Osun-Oshogbo Sacred Grove was registered as a UNESCO World Heritage Site. By that time I was deep into my work and glad that I had met at least the receding footprints of her world.

That night, I slept in Oshogbo in a room at the Nike Center for Art and Culture. Nike Olaniyi Davies, now Nike Davies Okundaye, an internationally celebrated artist opened her center in 1983 to encourage and create jobs for young artists, especially women, and to preserve traditions in Yoruba arts.

Nike is every bit a modern-day heroine. She was raised in Ogidi, a town forty kilometers from Lagos, where the Benue and Niger rivers meet. Ogidi is famous for its celebrated son, the author Chinua Achebe; for weaving and pottery; and for indigo, which is said to grow in abundance there. Nike's great-grandmother, Ibitola, or "Red Woman," was an *Iyalode*, one of the astute and enterprising businesswomen who held chieftaincy titles and influence in the local councils. In the 1950s Ibitola was the head of an important women's loom guild in Jos, a seat of power in central Nigeria. She had specialized in *ojas*, finely woven and designed baby carriers, but abandoned that work to make indigo *adire*, because of what she described as the even more intense labor of weaving. Nike grew up assisting her great-grandmother with the strenuous preparation of the cassava paste used in designing the cloth; it became a resist to the indigo bath.

She hand-tied and stitched designs on cloths—also a tedious, involved, and slow process—and did embroidery work for a local tailor.

After primary school, Nike was hired as a nanny and left her family home, an arrangement not unusual for girls of that age, whose families were unable or unwilling to continue their schooling. She continued to make *adire* cloths on the weekends, which her employer sold to Canadian visitors who admired her work. She reinvested her profits from these sales and sold more and more of the cloth.

When Nike's father arranged a marriage for her to a much older man, she and a friend ran away to escape. They joined a traveling theater, which led her to a life in Oshogbo. Yoruba traveling theaters were similar to the world of the Western circus of long ago. Troupe members were often viewed as outsiders or drawn there out of desperation, as much as a desire to perform. The troupe belonged to or "married" its creative master, who paid them low, irregular wages and often coerced members physically or sexually, manipulating the laws of polygamy. The female cast especially bore intense abuse and also disdain by the outside community, which often likened the girls to prostitutes. Nike eventually left the theater because of these hardships, and because her father had succeeded in tracking her and made increasingly stronger attempts to force her into the marriage.

In Oshogbo, Nike met Prince Twins Seven Seven, a member of the playwright Duro Lapido's theater company. He would eventually be introduced to Àdùnní

and Ulli Beier and became one of the most important, but wildly eccentric and volatile, personalities in
the Oshogbo School of Art. Nike married Twins in
an attempt to escape her father's pressure and over the
years their marriage was joined with eight other wives.
The household was violent and contentious, as the wives
competed for food and money and other basic resources,
as well as protection from Twins's abuses and excesses.
Twins relied on his wives to do the base work for his
painting and tapestries, and Nike, who was favored for
her work, and smart and adept in her relationships, used
her situation as an opportunity to shelter herself and
develop her skill with *adire* and with other artistic forms.
In interviews, she has talked of the abuse and forced
sexual relationships between the co-wives, and how it
fostered attachments between the women and allowed
them to consolidate their own power. As Twins began
to sell his work and travel internationally, he increasingly
relied on Nike, sometimes even sending her as his agent.
She slowly developed contacts with other artists and
patrons and buyers. By the time she escaped the marriage
(also assisting some of her co-wives in leaving), her own
art was receiving the same attention as the stars of the
Oshogbo movement.

But for the most part women were left out of the
Oshogbo movement. They were, on the whole, bound to
domestic duties and to supporting their children. Only
through contact with the work of individual women's
husbands did a very few catch the attention of Àdùnní,
Ulli Beier and his second wife, Georgina Beier, also an

important artist and figure in Oshogbo, and foreign agents and buyers. And then the Oshogbo artists, as a whole, were assigned the same stigma as traveling theater: they were branded as derelicts and mad persons and pagans in Yoruba society. For women, it meant an intense, if not unbearable, exile.

Nike's most celebrated and iconic works are elaborate wax paintings on fields of indigo, an art form she shares with Àdùnní. Her work can be found in the most important auction houses and museums worldwide, often sold alongside the works of Àdùnní and Twins Seven Seven.

The afternoon before I was to visit Nike's Center for Art and Culture, I was walking on the road in Oshogbo with my research assistant, Yinka, a graduate student in African studies at the University of Ibadan. Yinka spotted a former college classmate carrying a newborn and called to her. We talked for a long time at the roadside, and then Yinka's friend invited us to an apartment just down the road that was rather lavish but suffering somewhat from neglect, dust, and pollution. It turned out to be Twins Seven Seven's home, and the young woman was his newest wife. She could not have been thirty; the man would be nearing sixty, I calculated. The two of them reminisced in Yoruba in the tones they must have used as schoolgirls. I was trying to conjure Nike's life and imagined this young wife might offer me some look into her husband's world. But she seemed to have no further ambition beyond marriage to a man who could set her up in this house, no plans except babies; everything rested on her marriage and her beauty, which was already battered by motherhood. When their attention turned to me, Yinka told her about my work and my interest in the Oshogbo artists.

When we were leaving, she disappeared for a long time and returned to offer me a battered, unremarkable painting by Twins at an inflated price. She and I were both latecomers, guided by yearning for beauty belonging to long-ago lives. We said good-bye, and Yinka and I had hastened on.

Thousands of young artists have come to the Nike Center for Art and Culture for training by the few remaining old master artists, including a few of the *Iyalaros*, the masters of the indigo pot. The center was inspired by the work of Georgina Beier, also a textile artist, who, one by one, trained women and men in textile techniques, and she began feeding the Oshogbo arts movement.

Georgina drew on traditional Yoruba textile designs, then led artists to use imported materials like velvet. *Adire* designs on velvet, dyed in indigo, created intensely glowing wrappers and *geles* that became high fashion. Yoruba society seemed to have an insatiable taste for new things. Modern fashions in a Yoruba aesthetic easily became a rage. She also introduced quilting work, using European conventions on indigo *adire*. These quilts inspired exhibits and high-end sales to foreign visitors who flocked to Oshogbo and to exhibits abroad.

Nike took Georgina Beier's vision and expanded it. The original center is housed in a fancy compound and has a large boutique that sells Nike's and her students' work, as well as masterworks by other Yoruba textile artists. She has added centers in Lagos, Ojidi, and Abuja, Nigeria's new capital city—each compound more lavish.

Nike frequently shows her work abroad and is invited to arts and African studies conferences all over the world. I had met her in New York, where she charismatically held forth in a room of buyers and fans. She was not at the center when I arrived; now married to a former police chief, she lived primarily in Lagos and was at that moment traveling in Germany. But I hadn't really come to Oshogbo for Nike, as much as I considered her a heroine. I was aware of how remarkable her world was, glad to look in but not sure it was my path. I wanted to find of indigo what was hidden.

That night I slept under a hand-sewn indigo quilt I'd bought from Nike's shop, made from an exquisite old piece of Ibadandun, "Ibadan is sweet." My nose was filled with it, and it took me into a calm trance before sleep. Sleeping in the next room was Iyalaro Silifatu Àdùnní Suliman. She had arrived in the night from Ibadan, summoned by Nike's brother when I informed him of my quest. I was anxious to meet her; she was one of the remaining *iyalaros* whom Nike had invited to the center to teach.

The next morning I found Iyalaro in an *adire buba* and *iroin*, the same cloth tied at her head. She was sitting on the floor on a pile of white and aquamarine *sheddar*, a shiny, expensive damask cloth that was stiff from designs hand-painted on it in cassava paste. She had a quick smile, tiny eyes full of grace and humor, and high, full cheeks that, from her temples to the corners of her mouth, were crossed with the deep scars of the Yoruba. Her twin granddaughters, who were twelve or thirteen, dressed in matching rose-colored knit dresses with powder-blue knit hats, were at work with her, inspecting and folding yard after yard of cloth.

I sat with them and watched.

Iyalaro's mother came from a family of indigo dyers in Abeokuta, and she was named after a friend her mother admired, who took her as an apprentice when she was seven. She stayed with her namesake until she was fourteen. Later she married and joined her husband in Ibadan, where she trained in another well-known compound of *adire* dyers. In Yorubaland, guilds and their hierarchies were particularly strong; dyers usually worked in only one medium of design. Iyalaro was unusual because she'd been able to master and work in them all. She became a very significant dyer in Ibadan, specializing in the more unusual cloths, with names like "Four friends who know what to do," "I will sleep among the children," and "My wants are satisfied." "Nobody can see the depth of the ocean" is one of the most elaborate and beautiful designs—it was tied and stitched in great detail and was made only on commission. She became known for this cloth.

As the years passed, tastes changed, and demand for *adire* waned; work with indigo began to be thought of as "dirty work." Once a viable trade, fewer girls came to Iyalaro for apprenticeship. Her own daughter trained as a teacher. By 1992 Iyalaro no longer made *adire*. By then some felt nostalgia for indigo cloths, and there were efforts, like a weeklong Miss Adire Carnival in 1993, to revive people's passion for it, but it amounted to only a conventional pageant and fashion show. Its meaning slipped away, except among a small group of intellectuals and collectors. Years later Iyalaro was introduced to Nike, who invited her to teach at the center. Iyalaro, like Nike, began to travel abroad, teaching in museum and university programs on the lost art of indigo dyeing.

Iyalaro did a demonstration for me, laying out cloths in various stages of production. With chicken feathers and a bowl of cassava paste she sat with her granddaughters painting traditional designs on *sheddar*. She took me to the compound yard, where indigo pots, painted and decorated with cowries, were set up in a performance space. The pots were dry, but Iyalaro mimed the act of dyeing, and for a moment I felt like I'd landed in a Disneyland for the Yoruba arts. The place felt too aware of itself and an audience.

Iyalaro and the granddaughters and I could not communicate much. After a while Yinka's translations seemed obtrusive, and I told her not to bother. I followed Iyalaro's demonstration politely, no longer quite sure what I wanted, probably just her intense, quiet company. The technique did not really matter to me, because I was too bothered by the staging, by the dry dye pots, and it was after all well documented already. Ulli and Georgina Beier, some important historians and curators, members of the African studies faculty at Ibadan, and a group from the 1980s called Friends of Adire, had all done important work of archiving it for the tribe of the obsessed. I had hoped to touch the way of being of the artist, the cosmological and spiritual world of the dye pot, but I was beginning to realize it was a world I might never enter. And should I enter, the uninitiated, the stranger with time only to look and buy?

I was glad when the demonstration devolved into lunch and a wordless bonding as Iyalaro and I packed our things to travel together to Ibadan. She put on the clothing of purdah. We shared the front seats of the *molue*, or minibus, back to the city in quiet comfort. We said good-bye at the bus terminal, and the affection between us was clear. I got no cloth from her. We exchanged no addresses, made no promises, raised no expectations. I wanted only to breathe her air.

In Ibadan and Abeokuta I had visited some of the famous marketplaces for indigo cloth, like those at Oje and Itoku. Friends who had visited there, even in the early 1990s, had described them as a sea of blue and black and brown skin. Blue cloth was piled high, and indigo adorned most every body, bleeding into everything, sharp in your nose. I read once a NASA finding that indigo light has a wavelength of enough nanometers that it reaches far into space; I imagined that even from space, the cloth markets could be seen as shimmering blue points below. But only a few years later, these markets were full of imported laces and polyesters, sequined and embroidered velvets, and woven sets made of Lurex, jokingly called "Chinese plastic." They were electric, vulgar, wonderful cloths but the antithesis of the vernacular of blue.

I'd collected dyers' names from friends and scholarship on *adire* and brought the list with me. I decided to go first to one of the more important dyers, Alhaja Ajoke Soetan, who lived in Kemta in Abeokuta. My heart was racing as I neared the compound. I was not sure what I would find. According to the historical record, indigo once dripped everywhere, bled into everything here. Dyers' houses were said to be built on blue mud. The dye vat was used to color the *iyalaros'* houses.

In an open shed beside the large family house, I could see cloths hanging on a line, but the stink of chemicals told me they were not indigo. At the door of Alhaja's house I was greeted by a young girl. When I asked if it was her house, she smiled. She slowly swung open the screen door and stepped out, to stand with me and Yinka on the doorstep. It took me a minute to follow her cues. I looked at the white tiles at my feet, dusted with red earth. Alhaja's name was written on them. I was standing on her grave.

The women working in the compound were all older, their gray heads closely shorn. They wore long rubber gloves and cloths tied like aprons to protect themselves from the dye. The blue ran to dirty black and left a thick odor. The cloths they dyed had the simple designs you see replicated in every market. It left me broken-hearted and unable to ask the questions I wanted to ask. To thank them for inviting me to look in, I bought a piece of purple cloth with a wax design stenciled with a pattern from stiff polyester lace.

I went to other dyers on the list and was told of other deaths, in variations of the same scene.

*Adire* had always been the domain of women, except for the men who became stencil-cutters. They were responsible for cutting the designs used by the *iyalaros*, who favored stencil-work—popular with buyers and less labor intensive. The stencils were cut from the lead linings of European tea chests. Later, in the 1950s and 1960s, as styles that relied on stitching became the vogue, men dominated as machine stitchers. Indigo was, for the *iyalaros*, female traders, and those in some ancillary roles, a means to amass great wealth and even political power, as Nike's great-grandmother, Ibitola, had done.

Yoruba women were expected to be financially independent from their husbands. Men covered their wives' debts but had no control over their profits, which women used to support themselves and their children. They therefore lived under a strict code of both spousal obedience and independence. Indigo wealth had allowed women unprecedented power and autonomy. Indigo *adire* had once been big money. In 1936, for instance, the dyeing industry brought a quarter of a million pounds into Yorubaland. The colonial government recognized *adire* as a leading economy, which meant that women, for the first time, made significant inroads with both the colonial and the traditional structures of power. Yoruba indigo was exported as far away as Brazil, and *adire* cloth was traded rigorously as far as Senegal and Gabon. And *adire* was simply one of many Yoruba indigo cloths, popular but certainly not the most prestigious or valuable.

At the turn of the twentieth century, the introduction of chemical blues fatally undercut indigo wealth. The Russians had successfully synthesized blues in the eighteenth century, but it was the Germans who introduced synthetic indigo, Indigo Pure BASF, in 1897. Its originator, Johann Friedrich Wilhelm Adolf von Baeyer, had spent more than twenty years trying to unlock the science of indigo. For this and other innovations, he won the Nobel Prize in chemistry in 1905. Soon after World War II, the German companies BASF and ICI began to export chemical indigo. The blues were not as deep or tonal as natural indigo, nor was the dye completely fast, but dyers began to use it as an additive to natural indigo to quicken the process. In the 1960s BASF opened for business in Lagos.

For brief moments, like the era of the Oshogbo movement, some vigor returned to the indigo market. But for a number of reasons, totally organic indigo dyeing soon disappeared. For one thing, the process of indigo dyeing is tedious and slow. People must gather wild indigo leaves; pound and dry them into balls—up to 150 for a single vat—to set them to ferment and dry; collect ash and process it so that it acts both as a mordant for the cloth and as a solvent for the dye; prepare stencils or cassava paste, to use as a resist; and tie, pleat, fold, hand- or machine-stitch, or hand-draw elaborate designs into the cotton. It all takes many weeks of work. The *iyalaros* relied on a complex hierarchy to execute it: initiates of Iya Mapo and individual guilds performed specific tasks on specific kinds of *adire*; young girls, through a system of kinship, apprenticeship, indentureship, and slavery did the base design work. Greater work opportunities for women and access to girls' education were also contributing to the art's demise.

BASF's history reminded me of Vlisco's tactics with the Mama Benz. Yoruba women had always expressed a penchant for cosmopolitanism, for the new and modern. Even *adire* dyers, who seemed to market tradition, embraced rapid innovation and happily adopted new materials and designs. In fact, it was the import of shirting, and later heavy satin and velvet from Europe, that had spurred the *adire* industry, giving dyers who previously worked on woven hand-spun cotton a smoother, wider palette upon which to experiment.

And so when a certain Mr. Hoffman from BASF Lagos went to a famous Ibadan dyer, Madame Faderera, with a business proposal, and the two began to travel about, touting the new dyes, people responded excitedly. Madame Faderera was set up as a wholesaler. She organized tie-dye training workshops that anyone could attend, collapsing old hierarchies. At the same time she and BASF Lagos exercised a strict control over supplies and distribution. This step undercut the powerful trade unions of the *iyalaros* and put a large share of dyers' profits into male and foreign hands.

After Oshogbo I decided to leave Nigeria. I felt like I was there only as a collector, a tourist of the past. Talk of a petrol strike was brewing; Lagos was still edgy from a massacre on the day of my arrival. The roads felt like death arcades, with sudden collapsed craters, the hulking skeletons of vehicles burnt in crashes, electricity dancing along the power lines. Signboards erected by the government warned against the dangers of ritual murders and Christian cults. The buses were filled with itinerant evangelists who preached fervently for hours, then become hawkers of medicines. The specter of death was everywhere. But most of all I felt uneasy with myself. Everything was in decay, and I was standing in the midst of it, romantic for the past, with a satchel of loot. Àdùnní's eyes seemed to reach into me, pointing at my own dislocation. I decided to forgo fabled Ogidi, Nike's birthplace. I would approach the Hausa dye pits in Kano from the north later, when I journeyed to Niger.

Eurama would perform *faafo* the next week—the one-year rite when the soul of the dead is said to cease to roam freely and cross the river into the world of shadows. Eurama would end her public mourning and remove her mourning cloth. I felt pulled to return to Accra, where I was less of a stranger. And I had a special gift for her that I'd bought in Oshogbo: her first pair of blue jeans.

On the morning I was to leave for the airport, the petrol strike was on. The roads were mostly deserted, and as I sat outside my hosts' place, a man slipped into the car shed and siphoned gasoline from a neighbor's Mercedes-Benz. The newspaper, under the headlines about the strike, carried an article about a newly enacted ban on the import of all printed fabrics. Less than one quarter of the factories that were producing cloth in Nigeria a decade earlier were still in operation today. The minister of industry was leading a committee charged with making

Nigeria self-sufficient in textile production by 2006. It is a very old story, improbable propagandizing. The truth is that by 2006 Asian imports would nearly eclipse all other sales. And in the remotest parts of West Africa, Chinese agents, speaking not the languages of trade like Hausa or Mandingo but local dialects, would be selling pirated and machine copies, made in more than thirty Chinese factories, of every cloth precious to anyone. The men at Vlisco hoped that it would flatten the road for them to sell beyond their traditional markets, but in truth Dutch sales were down more than 30 percent.

That morning I sat with my host, Peju, at breakfast, telling her of my sorrow at arriving so late in Ibadan. She laughed and said, "Well, at least you found your family house!"

I didn't understand her.

"Don't you know that the *iyalaro*'s home that you visited yesterday was your professor's grandmother's place? His grandmother was a great woman, one of the most powerful, wonderful dyers."

I couldn't believe her! He had never told me. The cloth he had given me was only "something he'd collected" on a trip home, he'd said. Was it, like the others that hung in his home, one of her cloths? Why had he withheld this fact from me, even during all those years when my obsession with indigo grew, and as I headed off to his homeland? Was it a willful omission, or an inability to connect to something of his past? I had stood in his grandmother's compound without knowing that it was hallowed ground, the place that had set my journey flowing.

I paid a large sum in dollars to my host's driver to buy petrol to take me to Lagos. As he and I made the almost two-hour-long journey on empty roads, both of us were silent, aware of each other's anxious desire to reach our homes. I clutched a bag of cloth between my knees, wondering, again, at the folly of my obsession.

# Blue Gold and Concubines, Niger

Niger feels like a land of fire. The temperatures reach well above 107 degrees for much of the year. People move with a silent litheness, as if perpetually crossing something burning. The air has a cracking quality, as does cloth against the skin. Sweat evaporates as if an iron had been touched to it. From Niamey, Niger's capital, I boarded the twice-weekly bus for the journey north to Agadez, which would take more than a full day, wondering how the body calibrates. But there is a gentleness to the extreme, and you trust and dance into the fire.

I was traveling this time with four others—Afi, my Jewish-American and Ghanaian friend; another Fulbrighter, Julie, who was studying Ghanaian electoral politics, and Lindsay, an older woman who had lived and worked as a development consultant in the Volta region of Ghana for eight years. We were each on our own desert quest. I was excited to be journeying into L'Aïr Massif, the gateway to the trans-Saharan routes.

At early dawn, as we set off, a small herd of wild giraffes looked calmly into the window of our bus, which was stalled on the road leaving the city. What great fortune! it seemed.

Six hours into the journey, we reached Birnin Konni,

a small border town just a spit from Nigeria. Along the way I watched the road, weighing the prospect of dipping down to the Kano dye pits on my return to Agadez. The roads were desolate, and there were easier routes through Lagos and Abuja, but I wasn't sure I wanted to make such a long journey through Nigeria's south. I decided to leave it up to whim, and turned my thoughts to what was ahead, feeling excited and anxious.

It was August 2000, and we'd arrived at a moment of armistice in the decades-long Tuareg Rebellion raging between the Hausa-dominant south, the seat of government, which controlled profits from uranium mining in the Tuareg-dominated north (Niger is the world's fourth largest source), and the nomadic Tuareg, who emblemized Niger's rank at the time as the lowest on the Human Development Index. It was a fight over land rights, political power, and control of precious resources, some lucrative and others dwindling. It was also shadowed by the Tuaregs' role as conduits and raiders over many centuries in the trans-Saharan slave trade and as agents of the Islamic reform movement. It was difficult for me to read the air, to understand how sharp or how relaxed the tensions might be, but at a stop to refuel, halfway to Agadez, soldiers boarded our bus with semiautomatic rifles. They occupied the front seats and stuck the barrels of their guns out the bus windows, pointed up to the sky, a dramatic flag of defense. For the next twelve hours, on mostly deserted highways, the bus slowed and the soldiers warily inspected every nearing car or truck, every camel laid across the road, before signaling to the driver to continue on. Someone explained to us that ambushes were common and that camels, wild and domestic, roaming freely, were often rigged with explosives.

The heat rose, and the air became heavy with vapor. We crossed the moonlike terrain, passing small clusters of tiny adobe homes with miles between them, herds of sheep and goats, an occasional traveler on a loaded donkey, and as always, camels wandering unfettered. Amazingly, after almost thirty hours of motoring, we only just crossed the frontier before L'Aïr Massif, the frontier to the Sahara. These lands had long been plied by caravans headed south to Mali, Burkina Faso, Nigeria, and Ghana. On these modern routes indigo cloth from the Kotar Mafa pits in Kano is still transported north and west in a vigorous trade with the Tuareg, Bororo, and Wodaabe peoples.

Our first night in Agadez, we chose a guide purely on instinct, trusting his gentle spirit and desert-aged face. Sidi Mohamed was not yet thirty but the harsh climate had aged him so that he appeared to be middle aged. As he walked us to the outskirts of the city to the Tuareg *campement* where his mother lived, he moved adeptly as one with space and the land. The next morning we followed him to the camel market to rent an extra steed to his five, for our five-day journey.

At the tailor shop in the Agedez central market, we ordered typical Tuareg women's blouses and matching men's pants, sewn from soft black factory-spun cotton that was embroidered in white, spidery geometries. I was surprised at how cool they felt, creating shade for the body. In a stall next to the tailor shop, I bought a scarf to protect my head and face from the sun and blowing sands. And from a locked glass case at the back of the shop, I purchased a *taglemust*. The soft gauzy skin of it was wound tight and then wrapped in paper and bound with string, so that it was the size of a large ear of corn. When I opened it, the loose, metallic indigo powder, mixed with goat fat and beaten into the cloth with a wooden paddle by men in Kano who were part of a guild of beaters, sifted into my palms. It smelled rich and loamy, of the vat. As I unwound a stretch of it, it glistened blue-black-purple, and outside in the sun it turned glinty and radiant.

I tucked it into the bag I traveled with. I was afraid even to unwrap it and watch its power diffuse in the air as the powder dropped away. It was costly, nearly $80 for the simplest cloth, which was prohibitive for most Nigeriens. A *taglemust* of one hundred bands was considered the most elegant and expensive; this cloth was not half of this.

Men donned the *taglemust* at adulthood, after undergoing family and clan ritual and then seclusion, and then they wear the veil always. Tied to it are notions of vernacular, self-worth and respect, masks for vulnerability and shame. Donning it is an act of social distancing, a reminder of the need for caution and self-control with others. It hides emotion and allows men to maintain a restraint and highly constructed self-image. For women, it is a veil that does not hide the face but, for ceremonies, cascades from the head, weighted by beautifully embellished silver weights. That morning we had walked past the grand mosque at the call to prayers and watched a sea of men, most heads wrapped in indigo, filing in from the side streets, kneeling to the ground, resplendent. My body welled with longing to enter the depths of that collision of faith, feeling, history, and divine beauty.

At dawn the next day we were at the outskirts of Agadez. The camels were fitted with neon orange and green and pink factory-made blankets from China and then loaded with saddles hand made of turquoise and red and yellow leather, elaborately tooled. The camels protested and cursed, some eyed us with wariness, and finally they accepted our weight atop them. From a distance two Fulani men, tall and slender, watched us, their heads swathed in blue-black *taglemusts* that fell across their chests. One wore a dramatic, cone-shaped herdsman's hat atop it all, with three clusters of indigo-dyed ostrich feathers attached near the brim. Indigo and ostrich feathers—they had transversed the desert for centuries, traded all the way to northern Europe. The men carried proper European women's purses, the long straps wrapped around their wrists. Their mouths were stained blue, and their eyes looked piercingly at us, unmoving, and we stared back. They could not have been more beautiful, and they seemed aware of it, seemed to have made a pact to move in a pair, each complementing what the other had achieved. We gazed at each other, unembarrassed. "They think you and Afi are Tuareg," Sidi said, but they were not sure if Afi is a woman because she is so tall. Afi and I laughed; she was as tall and boyish as they were effete.

Just two weeks from now the Cure Salee, or Guérewol, would take place, the annual festival marking the beginning of the rainy season, when the ground is rich with salt for cattle to consume, and Tuareg and Wodaabe Fulani clans—both the camel and the Land Rover sets—travel from the Sahara to meet for a beauty pageant of Wodaabe men, a subgroup of the Fulani. Adorned with richly embroidered indigo and ostrich feathers, their faces made up with cosmetics derived from indigo and henna imported from Hausaland, and from sacred clays mined from deep in the desert, they perform a ball, competing for beauty and refinement, and for strength of body and countenance. The Guérewol, called just a few days after we arrived, would be held in In-Gall, three hours west of Agadez. The town of less than five hundred people would swell to tens of thousands for the weeks surrounding the festival. I could not stay so long, but these men were giving us a look into its pageantry.

The men finally met our smiles as the camels began to walk, slowly, toward the rising sun, into a landscape of depletion that became more haunting, more of a stunning moonscape the farther we ventured.

For five days we traveled from Agadez to Azzel, Issekah Seghan, Tassolam-Salant, Boughla, and then back to Agadez, in the overwhelming heat. Every part of us that touched the saddle was rubbed raw until it bled. The camels loped and lurched, spitting, kicking at times, protesting and humming. They are gormless creatures, these Ships of the Desert, but you trust in them completely and they become incredible to behold.

We would wake each morning with the first glint of sun and dig into the sand until we hit water. It would fill the hole, six inches, a foot, for bathing. Then we would travel in the early morning hours. The two men who served as *chameliers* for our guide would run beside us in the 110-degree heat, then suddenly drop back, disappearing sometimes for hours, then lope from behind a dip in a plateau and join us again.

We passed salt pits, where men with faces and clothes tattered by the harsh sun and wind labored to harvest the dirty cakes. We encountered occasional small caravans not much larger than our own, or single travelers, herders, all men with heads swathed and enormous swords crossed at the waist. The caravans passing the salt pits were but a faint memory of the ancient trade—once as far as the Roman Empire—in natron, a rare, naturally occurring mix of soda ash; bicarbonate, or baking soda; and salt, prized for its healing, cooking, cleaning, and medicinal uses, for nourishing livestock, and for its power as an agent in indigo dyeing. Natron was abundant in Egypt, in places in Niger, and on the shores of Lake Chad. Kano dyers, especially, coveted it; and the dye pits, the salt mines, and the caravans had each—to an extent—survived on their mutual dependency.

By the late morning, we would look for a shady spot to rest—often only low brush. We would lay blankets in it and keep our bodies still, amazed at how even dappled shade offered a decadent cool. The breeze seemed to pick up, as we slept and listened to the men tell stories in Tamashek. At nightfall, as if by a miracle, we would arrive at an oasis, a palm-covered grove where fresh dates grew and well water flowed, and we would drink downstream from our foul-mouthed steeds. We were supplicants to their strength, their intuition, their instinct always to survive, and their patience carrying us along. At night we slept beside them until they wandered off near morning.

On the third day, behind a caravan of four-wheel drives, we arrived at a settled area in an oasis, with concrete houses and small stores. We surprised a desert wedding, with throngs of Tuareg women clad in indigo veils over indigo dresses embroidered deep red, or in white blouses adorned with sequins, each displaying their heavy dowry gold over hands and faces patterned with blue-black lines. The bride was hidden in the center of them, and the men stood on the perimeter, leaning against the cars. They sang and clapped, and their feet beat the ground like the wings of birds. They seemed to have a shifting quality, first like fire, the blue brilliance of flames, then like smoke, ephemeral. I felt their substance, and yet they were substance-less, because they were only a glimmer in my eye, and then we were gone, as swiftly and completely as the *chameliers*, leagues of sand between us and them.

Back in Agadez, we boarded a bush taxi, a small minivan, to In-Gall, the site of the Guérewol, to see what kind of festival preparations had begun in that town built on a remote oasis.

The road seemed utterly deserted except for wandering

animals. Then the heat rose, and people appeared seemingly out of the air, and the minivan stopped to admit others to the crush of bodies. I feared we'd be asphyxiated. The man across from me was so close that the indigo of his *taglemust* stained the shoulder and sleeve of my dress, and our faces collided whenever we hit a pothole. Another man sat and played with Afi's bracelet, turning it, and pointed out camels as they passed. A third slept against me, staining my other side. He was ivory skinned, bone thin, elegant, with eyes like small pumpkin seeds. Indigo leached into the men's hands and faces and clothes. I thought of Eurama's warning: *"Take care, or you will run off with one!"* I laughed. One of my friends had already made plans to stay on with Sidi Mohamed. I simply wanted the ride to go on long enough that I was bathed in indigo.

In-Gall was a sleepy town, just beginning to wake with preparations. We slept the night there, on mats laid in our host's yard. Every year for centuries, at the time of the Guérewol, the caravans would come in from points as far as three thousand miles into the desert, to rest, to indulge, and to find human company. For those transporting indigo, it was the moment when a blue wealth was material.

The bus I rode back to Niamey was packed with so much weight that its roof was caving. The luggage racks above our seats had been soldered again and again and seemed on the verge of breaking for the last time. With every bump, the roof would press down under the weight.

People slept, babies stood and played on women's laps, sometimes knocked down. I sat tense, wondering, did someone worry that this bus of mostly women would be crushed, or did they expect we simply hold the load on our heads?

This time the bus traveled for a while along the southern border and dipped into Nigeria a few times. I decided to forgo Kano. It was not the right time.

The Hausa-controlled Kotar Mafa pits of Kano date back to the late 1400s. They are the oldest still-active dye pits in West Africa, close to the original palace of the emir, who established for his successors centuries of wealth. In Kano there were hundreds of remaining pits, but most were rumored to have fallen into disrepair, clogged with stones and refuse. Not even the Saharan sales could revive their past.

The Hausa kingdom of Kano was established before 1000 A.D., but its popular record conceals a five-hundred-year legacy of concubinage of women raided in acts of war against the west and south. As concubines, these women surprisingly controlled the original dye pits and their profits, and used indigo cloth as currency, circulating it among regional courts and the powerful. They had the power to assess state taxes, the primary one being grain. And they became the territorial representatives of the Emir from the areas in which they were captured, extending their power, which they shared with their children who—under Islamic law—were free and had the agency to become royals.

The concubines' power was eventually wrested from

them under the Kano Emirate, formed in 1805. The emirs overtly pursued commercial dyeing themselves, despite ancient ideas about indigo dyeing and its mimicking of birth and deep-held taboos about male contact with the dye pot. Indigo was effectively turned over to the Malams, the Koranic teachers, and Kura, the district in Kano that is the site of the dye pits, became thereafter a city of men. By the early 1900s there were an estimated twelve thousand dyers overseeing fifty thousand active pits.

I would leave Kano for another time. Senegal was calling.

# ELEVEN

# Divine Sky, Senegal and New York City

I went to St. Louis, a peninsular town in northern Senegal that touches the border of Mauritania, in search of a fabled cloth—an indigo of unrivaled luxury and refinement, of stunning handwork. This cloth is a love song to both the turbulence (if not the violence) and the beauty of *métissage*, the mixing of the races. This cloth has its origins in the Cape Verde Islands, some five hundred miles off the Senegalese coast, on the plantations the Portuguese established in the sixteenth century to feed their renowned cotton textiles to European markets, a trade that flourished through the eighteenth century. Skilled slaves, primarily women but also persons working with contracts, were brought from the mainland to the previously unpopulated islands for the purpose of weaving and dyeing. The Portuguese eventually introduced Japanese patterning to the workshops (the precolonial and colonial history of Asian-African exchange is largely unexplored) and in instances actual artisans from Japan were imported. In needlework so fine that it can be better characterized as embroidery, these women and men stitched signs and symbols that were a collision of Moorish, Iberian-Islamic, Arab, Japanese, Wolof, Soninke, and other African cultures. Photos of the cloths, which I've seen in colonial sketches and vintage postcards from the late 1800s and the turn of the century, show midnight-colored indigo, the work of master dyers able to achieve a rare alchemy in the vat. In the photos wealthy women sit wide-legged, adorned with layers of the cloth to accentuate the twins of prestige, cloth and girth. The white resist patterning covers their bodies like a script. These women were of a culture of opulence, the wives and concubines of wealthy traders. Many others were the descendants of *signares*, bourgeois Franco-American women entrepreneurs. Their merchant community, in the seventeenth and eighteenth centuries, controlled trade in the region, exercising ties with the Catholic Church to protect their interests in colonial administration and the European trade in slaves, gum arabic, and beeswax. St. Louis had been the capital of the French colony of Senegal from 1673, but with the introduction of the steamship, a railroad, and increasing French investments, merchants and government in Dakar slowly wrestled political and economic control from St. Louis. Still the legend of the *signares* lives on in the cloth.

I fell in love with St. Louis, whose old city is centered on a finger of land—the Langue de Barbarie—between the Atlantic coast and the estuary of the Senegal River. In just a short walk, you can traverse ocean, Langue, and river and cross the wild marshes of the mainland into the Sahel. The searing noon heat gives way to the nighttime cold of the Harmattan that chases you into wool sweaters. You can enjoy ice cream in an Internet café as brilliant painted horse-driven chariots thunder by with modern grandes dames, wearing heavy gold and cloth that mimics the opulence of the past. In the marina, fancy motorboats are moored, and behind them, at the beach, are brilliantly painted fishermen's canoes. The city's riotous *métissage*—of people, of land—pulled sharply at me. The cloth, which contains that same inheritance, with such beauty and sophistication, became a symbol of the riot in me.

At the few antiques shops in town, I inquired about the cloth. Some sold Mauritanian blues—five-meter-long gauzy fabric, some with similar patterning, and deep blue-stained details. But everyone admitted that old indigo cloths were not easily found, and fewer were bought and sold. The families who had them knew their value as heirlooms, as part of the story of the clan and of St. Louis.

I'd accepted that I was on an obsessive search, and that a kind of drunkenness propelled me to the *quartier ancien*. I began going house to house, entering one yard after another, with no language, really, only a photograph of the cloth. Mostly I was shrugged off by families amused by my searching or unwilling to entertain me.

The Soninke peoples say that when a family went to a dyer to commission a cloth, they were asked to choose a color of the sky above them. That day, I watched dark clouds roll overhead, and I nearly abandoned my search until a man from a house I'd visited called to me and led me back to his yard. Two women stood in the compound with two very old, brilliant shawls, shouting at each other and drawing a crowd of those who would be peacemakers and others taking sides. The matriarch of the house stood in a doorway, looking sadly on, seeming to choose reserve. I sat dumbly by, knowing I should leave, knowing that it was even more vulgar than the incident in Makola with the *taglemust* for me to sit there, amid the explosion, caring only about this cloth. I didn't really know what they were fighting over. I wanted to convince myself that what was at stake was mere recreation; you find wild feuds among bored, frustrated family members in many a compound. But I felt a terrible struggle. Could I just walk away? Was having this cloth a gesture at the sublime, as I'd convinced myself, the literal last threads of something handed over for another's caretaking? Or was it simply my insatiable desire, my drunken need? Each cloth that was folded in my cloth box was a thing of uncommon beauty, but I was aware that I was no closer to spirit or to the human closeness I sought.

When I left the compound, it was with one of the shawls folded in my bag, the fight trailing behind. It was close to a century old, pristine dark beauty with white telegraphed designs. It represented something of me; it was the insistence that I had come to the end of my journeying.

"All the beautiful ones!" Eurama said, holding the cloth across her when I returned to Accra. "What more now? Tell us, Madame Blue!"

"You know Mali," he said. "You know the one bridge in Bamako that takes you across the Niger River into the center of the city? When we were young, as the rainy season began, we would stand on that bridge and watch the hippos migrate upriver. They would come in herds, and they are very dangerous, but we could safely watch them. As I grew, they became fewer, and when I returned to Bamako from France when I was eighteen, after just seven years, they had nearly disappeared.

"We would go to the river, and women would do their dyeing there. Everyone used the river for their work to save on their water bills. They would wash the cloths, straight from buckets with caustic soda, an agent to speed the dye process. You would see fish floating dead in the river where they had been.

"Growing up, I would spend my summer vacations in Guinea. My aunts were dyers, and one day my small cousin took a stone of caustic soda and swallowed it. It totally destroyed her stomach. She had to feed with a tube, and the family had to send her to France for more than five surgeries.

"But even before this I became fascinated with natural dyes and with indigo especially. I was fascinated with plants and the idea that you could extract colors from them. I learned a lot about plants in Guinea. Grown-ups would send us kids to collect things in the bush for medicine and for dyes. When I was seven, an old lady told me about indigo; I knew that it was used for medicine, for body aches, and for eye infections. But when I learned that it was used as a dye, I thought it was unbelievable that color could come from that plant."

I had met Aboubakar Fofana on the floor of ABC Carpet & Home, a famous high-end store in New York

City, one winter afternoon after I returned home. A tall, slim man with long dreadlocks and soulful eyes, he had the intense calm of the Sufi devotee and the look of the French bohemian in his tweed jacket and corduroys, antique Dogon jewelry, and indigo scarf he'd embroidered and dyed. We stood talking near a display of his work on the main floor, amid holiday shoppers. I was fascinated both with his beauty and with the $1,000-to-$2,500 scarves and throws that he made from organic cotton, grown on his land in Mali. The fabric was handspun and hand-woven, then surrendered to the vat in his Bamako studio. The most costly cloth was a heavy shawl called a Dissa, with long, beautiful fringe; it was dyed the blue-black shade called Lomassa, or "Divine Sky," the deepest color achieved by the master dyer. In ancient Mali, among the Soninke, the Dissa is extremely valuable, worth the cost of several cows. Aboubakar was interested in the idea of an African luxury market, something that has always existed but that the West has overlooked and that Africans, whose desires turned to Western modernism devalued. At the same time, he wanted to restore the tradition and "lost memory" of the creations of the Soninke masters, his own forebears, the renowned masters of weaving and dyeing in West Africa. Traditionally, at the birth of a male, mothers began the thread-making, the spinning of cotton, and the weaving of the Dissa, which would be given to the son at marriage, the advent of manhood. When the man died, the cloth would become his shroud, and the indigo would help transport his soul to the afterworld.

Aboubakar's father, a diamond dealer, died when he was young, and his mother, a merchant who traded through West and Central Africa, sent him to live with an uncle in Paris when he was eleven. His uncle was a TV actor who had married a French woman, and in his house Aboubakar suffered the pains of exile, French racism, and his uncle's neglect and violence and forced domestic work. He eventually ran away from his uncle's house and lived on the streets for several years, until a friend of his uncle's wife, a French woman who had always been kind to him, insisted he come to her house.

The woman provided him with safety, and something opened, he explained. He needed to express something inside of him.

"I started to think about art when I was fifteen years old. My father always said, 'Man must make an education.' I was the only boy in my family. In Mali I had been very spoiled, but I knew I had to make my own way now." He began to draw and went to night school to study ceramics and sketching. "I began learning calligraphy then. I really needed a discipline," he said, because the vagaries and dangers of Paris were taking over.

With calligraphy, he became fascinated with the idea of "putting one's life inside the strokes." It became the same thing with indigo: "Your being is in that vat." Aboubakar studied indigo in books, remembering what he'd learned as a child about the bush. He became "obsessed with the impossibility of things. How did blue come from these leaves?" Calligraphy had taught him that language was an art and not an exact science. When he read formulas of indigo, none were the same. He took from them the idea that the dye vat held living organisms requiring care and understanding.

"It was not intellectual, not a science. At that age, I was a big baby who missed love. This suggested something deeper, something of the spirit, and I became more obsessed with it."

When he returned to Mali after seven years, he traveled around the country and to Burkina Faso, Ivory Coast, and to Guinea, where he encountered indigo. "I took a trip to Dogon. Dogon is the site of the earliest identified woven African textile—a hat with indigo-dyed threads from the eleventh century worn by the Tellem peoples, the original inhabitants of what is now Dogonland. The women there were using chemical dyes and balls of indigo in the same vat. I had tried growing a vat by then—you literally grow organisms to get indigo dye—but it did not work." The mystery and seeming impossibility and his awareness of the erosion of Mali's environment and ancient cultures drove him even harder.

He returned to France and began working as a freelance graphic designer for large advertising companies. He married and had children, but he continued to be drawn back to Dogon country. "I returned there many times, and I would argue with the women about using a chemical process. Twenty years ago you could find many dye pots, but they were already using caustic soda and synthetic powders. Today you can hardly find a dye pot. It's too hard to get dark colors without synthetic agents, they would argue. Many of the women didn't know how to use the vat correctly. They were more interested in making cloths quickly so that they could get profits for each five-day market. They thought I was stupid. Some of them, at the end of all my talking, would ask me to bring a barrel of synthetic dye to make money."

By then Aboubakar was beginning to have success with the dye pot, and he was having success in France as a calligrapher and an artist. He got a foundation grant to study in Japan with the master dyer, Masakazu Akiyama.

Today he lives between France and Mali, where he has started an initiative for organic farming. It could be argued that he is the only person living in West Africa who practices a wholly natural, wholly organic dye process rooted in ancient technique, which he flexes with Japanese knowledge.

"I have one woman who helps me who can do the whole process. She really understands indigo. She was working as a washerwoman when we met, and my family would pay her to bring water from well. I began to train her to wash the cloths from the dye pot; they require special care and washing. After seven years she understands it; indigo is inside her. I can trust her with everything.

"The vats are my children. I name each one, names from our spiritual tradition. You know, there truly is life inside indigo. You have to learn a respect for that life. It depends on faith. The interaction with the dye pot is like an interaction with faith. It took me many years to understand and master this. You are in a relationship with that life. These organisms—I know all their needs.

I need to hear them to know what they need and then they can give me all the beautiful things that I need. You interact with the dye pot with an ultimate trust and pure heart. With indigo, I feel like someone who is honest. I feel no conflict in myself, just completeness, and I am far away from everything of the world. As much as I care for them, they adopt me.

"Every time I begin a new vat, it's like the first time, and I become really proud at the end of the life of the vat. The last shades are a very light blue, called 'blue *naissance.*' Blue birth. It is the color of a bluish eggshell.

"The freshness of the color at the end of the vat gives me goose bumps, something like a first memory. I feel like I gave the vat the best—everything. It is the happiest time for me, but also a kind of mourning."

Aboubakar told me that many times he killed the vat, which lives with a delicate alchemy, and mourned his lack of attention to something—the wrong balance of heat and light, a moment of inattention, tainted water or something else that might disturb the vat's alkaline balance. "Indigo teaches me to be humble in life. There is something bigger and taller than me; I am nothing. How can so much beauty and hugeness come from that tiny leaf? It is like trying to understand God—you cannot in a lifetime understand everything of indigo. You cannot really put words to the emotion. I'm looking for my own shades inside of these blues. I'm sure I cannot ever find them. When I find them, I will no longer have interest. When I find them, I will die.

"*Marabout* is a title that carries a lot of negative

assumptions—but my spiritual father is a *marabout* for lack of a better word. My parents were both followers, disciples of a great medicine man, a *marabout*. He taught them much about plant medicine and cosmology. My mother was a modern woman; she fed me with Similac and not the breast. She and my father had a fancy car, a high life. But they were followers. My teacher was also his disciple. He tells me, "God is the father of the fatherless. Indigo is the mother and father. Dream. Target. And love."

Indigo is love.

# Part III

# THE TASTE OF LIFE

# TWELVE

# It's Never Late, New York City

Accra farewells are so intimate. You leave your beloved at the airport, and in the middle of the big city, if you are near the coast and the flow of air traffic, pick that very plane out overhead. The roaring sky and exhaust are a long reprise on your good-bye. From the plane, I looked out my window and could mark the yellow glare of the Irish pub just before the junction at Eurama's. I knew that she and Lady Diana would be sitting in the shop, Senam the tailor across from her, and they would run into the street to wave at me passing overhead.

"My dear, stop all of this cloth cloth cloth! You have every cloth in the world. Even the beautiful ones, you now have them!" Eurama had said as I stood with her at the airport with all my anxious booty, packed into bags and a trunk—a large black metal box painted with red crescents that many women used to store their cloth. Her kids had taken it to Kojo Signwriter and had "Yaa McKinley"—Yaa the name for a Thursday-born child—emblazoned near the lock. As we packed my things into the car, she and her sisters and some of the area women offered a litany of advice: how to eat and stay slim; how to handle my money so that I could continue to care for Kwale, who was now enrolled in school and living full time at Eurama's; how to conduct myself back in New York now that I had some blue sense; and how not to disappoint them by becoming a stranger again.

"You could not be more a part of us. We are your family. Whatever you don't have in America, you have it in Ghana! You have to settle down. Stop all of this restless journeying. It's time for you to have a child—even just one child—so that you can finally taste life. I beg-o! Then you bring us that child, and we will put it at our back and carry it! I would love to carry your baby! But I want to feel like these our prayers for its very hardheaded mother, who lacks patience but not beautiful things, have been heard."

From Accra you fly in a long arc, northwest over the Sahara. As the hours progressed, I watched the line on the map on the screen slowly grow long. From Bamako to Kayes in Mali. To Nouakchott, Mauritania. Morocco. Then suddenly we seemed to be flying with absurd speed north toward Scotland.

I tried to settle into sleep, to force myself to surrender to being flung across space and into a kind of mourning. What would it mean to live at home in New York now, without Eurama and my people in Accra, without daily cloth and its stimulation in the eye, without being a part of others in the way I'd finally stitched together *communitas*.

As soon as I settled against the armrest, I heard a tense whisper: *"Owufo!"*

Farther up the aisle, a stewardess tore the plastic cover and unfurled a Ghana Airways blanket. She settled it over a man I'd watched all morning, handsome, dignified in his suit and bowler hat, a style Ewe men favored, bent over in a wheelchair that his daughter was pushing. Our departure had been delayed for nearly eight hours, the plane held by the Saudi government for clearance of funds. I had checked my bags and gone to Makola with Eurama to do her shopping, and come back to find him sitting in the same position.

The Westerners aboard the plane were oblivious to the death until we landed at Kennedy Airport many hours later and the plane was held to await a police inquiry. But unable to sleep, I had sat up, aware of the whispered comforts and sympathies, the benedictions passed around. I clutched a bag with my feet; it held my most precious indigo, among them mourning cloths. His death seemed another reprise on my journeying. I had often worried that I was courting death by collecting them. Perhaps it was a bit of magical thinking, but what did his death now mean?

One day soon after my return I traveled to Stamford, Connecticut, to visit my grandmother. When I alighted from a taxi, I saw her at the top of the long stairs up to the house surveying spots of ice. She didn't hear well, didn't notice that my car had arrived, and I stood looking at her. The house was forested by white birch trees and cedars as red-brown as West African earth; the weak sun filtered a white-gray light so that everything appeared blanched; and her white skin, white curls, and white wool hat disappeared into the tableau. The deep blue mohair coat she wore looked set ablaze.

In the weeks after returning home, I felt like I lived with stunned senses. I was starved for color and visual complexity as I walked the desolate streets, a feeling as acute as my loneliness for human company. I had seen my grandmother in that coat, in that pale winter landscape, many times before. The coat was part of the iconography of my childhood, of her life commuting to New York City where she ran her late husband's elevator company. I realized then that it was something about that figure, and the contrasts of starkness and blue fire, that I had probably always been seeking, both in cloth and in human attachments.

My phone rang, and she heard its low pitch and looked up at me. I waved to her as Eurama's voice carried from the phone.

"One Alhaji Taiwo arrived here this very early morning. I heard water in the pipes, and I was at the tap filling buckets. Everyone in the house was asleep. I saw this dirty traveler over the wall, and I was worried, Papa! I said, 'Ah, what four A.M. news is this? It is only death at this hour.' He said he was from Ibadan. Your friend Peju gave him directions to my place. You know these Nigerians, they can *travel*. He wouldn't stay; he wouldn't let me boil water for tea. So, anyway, my dear, your indigo is in. There is a note in it from Peju. I'll wait and see who is coming to your end and send it to you."

My grandmother stood watching me, smiling. "Well, look at you! You've come back; we've probably only lost the African half of you!"

*     *     *

Two months later, in the depth of a winter storm, I trekked from Hell's Kitchen out to Red Hook, Brooklyn, to a convent, to meet the sister of a woman whom Eurama had met and who received the parcel from a visitor in Accra from Tulsa.

Packed between ground cassava for eating and a bottle of Eurama's famous *shitor* pepper was an exquisite cloth. Folded inside of a brilliant treasure—a piece of old *adire* that the cloth seller at the University of Ibadan guesthouse had given to Peju, a regular at the club, for me—was a blue and white Vlisco cloth, designed with a pattern of lovely round disks.

"You know this one:'It's Never Late,'" Eurama told me when I called. "That one is for your baby! Hurry up and have one so you don't disappoint me."

My son was eight weeks old when Eurama arrived to "bath for him." Standing in my living room, she wrapped him in his cloth and put on the gold jewelry she had ordered. White waist beads to measure how he was growing, to hold his diapers, were instead wound on my wrist, confounded by Pampers. We put honey on his lips, then salt, representing life's sweetness, its coarseness, and whispered his name to him.

"Oh, *obruni!* You need to give him a proper ceremony!"

She was the first to put him on her back, to ease him into being carried. She stayed on until he was three months old, doing the work of a grandmother.

And when my daughter was born two years and a month later, I talked to Eurama in Accra from the hospital.

"*Ayeeko!* Well done. Now you are fully mother! You have two children for America and this our Kwale for Ghana. Hei! I forgot to tell you! She is menstruating. I took some of the money you sent and I've bought her first cloth. Imagine!"

She laughed when she told me that she was on her way to a family meeting for an aunt who had died. "I'm wearing the jeans you gave me. They are going to say America has spoiled me, but I won't mind them!"

One morning I awoke at dawn to my daughter's cries, fed her, and began the day, but by seven-thirty A.M., I was overcome with fatigue, teetering. I collapsed into a deep sleep, leaving the children to their father, oblivious to everything until the phone rang at 8:05.

"It's not good," my grandmother's caretaker, Abena, said.

I bathed quickly, carried my daughter on my back, left my son with his father, and took the train to Stamford. When I arrived, I walked past the priest and my grandmother's neighborhood friends to the bedroom, impatient with the ceremony, the greetings. My grandmother lay on her bed, in a nightgown. The bed was made up as it would be in Ghana, with layers of lace-edged sheets. A shock of white hair stuck out at the crown from beneath the belt of her terrycloth bathrobe, tied neatly near her ear, holding her mouth closed.

No one much dies at home anymore in America, not as a plan. I knew she was going but had left for the night, hoping that I would be able to return the next morning, or that my mother would arrive from Vermont before it happened. I could hear the wind escaping her, her hands felt like they had become only bone, and I hoped that she would be without us for only a few hours. I could not stay—I had my children with me. My daughter was just three months old, and she had been born with a cleft lip and palate, a rift in the continents of flesh that make up her face. She needed care that I could give her only at home.

Suddenly I felt very capable, adept, taking on the will of the women I'd known in Accra, making calls to family members and to the funeral home and police while I nursed my daughter.

In West Africa mourners gather to witness the end of a life. They embrace the head and begin to pour liquor and herbs into the body even as the person is dying, to give them comfort and preserve the corpse. I felt guilty that I had not been there to ease my grandmother's way, that I did not let myself openly love her and allow her to know she was mourned right until she slipped away. She died as singly as she had lived.

Out in the yard, my mother, who arrived too late, stood tearless and quiet under the rush of breeze in the cedar trees that my grandmother had loved and had seemed a part of. She had spoken about them even as she was dying. The body, encased, sterile, was lifted into the undertaker's SUV pulled up onto the lawn. We would not encounter it again until it was burned down to ash.

As the body was being taken out, Abena sat in the kitchen eating sardines and *kenkey*. *Kenkey* is eaten with the hands, and it had repulsed my grandmother, causing her to lash out about "people" and "their mouths." "What is it that you find so great about these Africans?" my grandmother demanded.

I brought my daughter to Abena and asked her to hold her, and she let me know she was annoyed by the interruption. She was tired and hadn't eaten since dawn. She followed me to the porch with my daughter in her arms, not realizing what was happening, surprised the body could be removed so quickly, within a few hours of her dying, so unceremoniously, with no witnesses, no real sending off, just the smooth wheeling away of a trolley.

Standing with her again, I was angry at my mother, for what I decided was her cowardice. She had not dropped everything and come as soon as I told her we were losing Grandmother. She had second-guessed me and said she would come the next morning, while I urged her to get right into her car. But then I thought, of course, perhaps she needed a community, midwives of death to pull her through to the burial, and later the labor of mourning, just as my grandmother had needed us to help hand her to death. Just as my mother had shakingly held my foot in the short-staffed labor room as my son was born, just as Eurama had uneasily held the foot of her husband.

"I always thought this was the best way, without all the pomp and circumstance," my mother said into the silence of the yard.

Abena's keening broke the calm. "Yei! Yei! Yei!" echoed down into the valley below the house, where you rarely heard any human noise except the occasional drone of a lawnmower. This was a place of retreat, of ex-*communitas*, the house my grandparents had built, where my grand- mother never pulled the blinds to the dark forest around her but lived in solitude from her early forties until she was ninety-eight. Abena's keening grew, and then was cut short, as if she became aware of its intrusion.

Two weeks later, in a quiet ceremony, we laid her ashes beside her husband's, eulogized her at the church, and went home for a meal with church friends distant to all of us, and that afternoon we began the task of dividing her things. We each supplied lists of what we hoped we'd take, and some began to mark art and furniture with Post-Its. The next morning most of us left, to mourn privately, to make meaning of the loss. African funer- als were labored with meaning I decided; ours too often were devoid.

When I had walked into my grandmother's bedroom and encountered her body there, my first impulse had been to get my camera from my bag. I felt like a thief, nervously returning to the closet where I'd left my bag, hiding the camera after I snapped a photo of her. A few days before the burial I made a guilty confession to my mother and gave her a copy of the photo, offering to share it with the family. I wondered about this shame. My mother and I had been the only ones to witness the body; she had transformed from a person to a body longer and leaner than we'd known, her skin whiter, her features sharp and beautiful in a new way.

I realized, having this photo, that I liked the corpse. I liked the reckoning with the body. I like that people can be as capable with it as they are with the body of the newborn.

One afternoon many months later, I tied my daughter on my back, put on some music, and danced her to sleep in my living room. Both of us were tired from the work of bringing two continents of flesh together, of helping her to grow bone. Work done in the womb was now done on the outside; her face grew beautifully as we prepared for the surgeries ahead. Repairing cleft under treatment with her doctors at NYU Hospital was like indigo dyeing: more magic, more art, than science. Each day I molded her face, fastening to her skin an architecture of tape, fastening a prosthetic mouthpiece to it with rubber bands, and calibrating the pull on the bone. I became an *Iyalaro*, the Mother of Tape and Rubber Bands; I talked to the spirits of bone and muscle and cartilage, as my daughter's face developed like a Polaroid photo each week for six months until her first surgery.

My children are my toil and my earthly sublime. I understood now Eurama's urging.

The music was a CD I'd bought long ago in Accra and never listened to. I'd mistaken it for old highlife music of the 1970s, but the sounds of Ga funeral dirges—joyous, aching, rhythmic songs—filled our home. As we danced, the tears spilled out of me. The songs were surrogates and lubricants for my own mourning, as those Accra funerals had been. It is hard to mourn alone, to let yourself stand at the wide open door of death. But once you "taste life" and approach your fear, you allow yourself to turn in.

I danced and danced, and when the phone rang, and I

heard my mother's voice, I let the music play a bit longer, hoping it might reach into her too.

"Your grandmother's bed belonged to her friend Helena. You know she has died, and the family has no use for it, but it is a very expensive bed. Can you think of anyone who can use it?" she asked.

Helena had been my grandmother's beloved friend. So connected were they that her son had lived for a time, with his Dutch wife, in my grandmother's basement, as he worked to establish himself in business and start a family.

"Her son is just retired as the head of Unilever Global, you know."

I started to laugh. Unilever. The king of soap and margarine in West Africa and former owner of Vlisco. Unilever, that had swallowed indigo.

My grandmother, who had never understood my pull toward Africa or believed that its history was at all tied to our own, had died on a bed that Unilever had bought. When she died, a lot of her comfort—the bed and Abena—had come from Africa.

How near our lives are to Africa; how strong and intertwined the threads. The world, and the history it makes, is really round, as the saying goes. And it is blue.

Years after I'd done my journeying, I discovered a Liberian folk tale about indigo from a collection of stories by the American artist Esther Warner Dendel.

In this story, the woman of legend is named Asi. Asi lived in a land of no hunger. Food was abundant, and when people were hungry, they could even eat the sky in little bits. With a scrap of cloud inside of you, a person could float and dream and find again the peaceful, joyous feelings that filled you, before High God left the earth to find peace from human comings and goings.

The people, in their loneliness for God, made sacrifices to the spirits of the ancestors and gave them messages to carry to God. Asi was one of the water people, a seeress and medium. The water spirits wanted Asi among them, and to appease them and calm their powerful pull, she had to make sacrifices to them with each full moon.

One day Asi went to the shrine at the bend of the river with her child tied at her back in a wrapper made of white cloth, a bag of rice balanced on her head. She would cook and eat some of her offering from the sacred spot and leave the rest to the spirits. She made a bed of leaves and laid her child there on her cloth to sleep. As she worked, she saw the color of the sky reflected in the river and felt hunger for that color. She imagined, as she ate a piece of the sky, that the color might come into her. She knew she was forbidden to ask for anything for herself alone, and not for the whole village, at the sacred pools. She knew she must beg forgiveness. But the feeling from the sky was so good, and she felt so drowsy and floating, that she ate more and more of it.

Asi awoke to the smell of scorched rice. The spirits would be angry with her; she had spoiled the sacrifice she'd come to make. She looked for her child and she saw that she had wet the bed and rolled off into the tall grass that grew nearby. The grass had smothered the child. Asi knew that she had been punished for what she had done.

Asi wailed in sorrow and covered her hair with ash from the fire, as is the custom for mourners. She picked up her child. Then she noticed that the cloth it had lain on was colored with a patch of bright blue. Just then she fell unconscious with grief, and in her dreams the water spirits came to her and revealed that the mixing of the salt of her tears, urine, river water, ash, and the wild indigo leaves that she'd plucked to cushion her child were the secret to God's earthly blues. It had been necessary for the child to die to have had this secret revealed to her.

The water spirits had taken her child; Asi was no longer held by them. She was ordered to guard her secret, to teach the old women how to make blue "go for down" and stay. She was to teach them the secrets of indigo. Only then would she again conceive and have her child's spirit returned to her.

High God, hearing of this affair, pulled the sky up even higher, where no one could break it off. And people look to the blue of fine cloth and have less need for High God, though in their hearts they remain lonely.

And indigo is here to stay.

I live now in blue, with my children, in a life fashioned between New York and West Africa, learning, as Eurama insisted, to really "taste life," through devotion to others, through the beauty of acts of sacrifice.

ACKNOWLEDGMENTS

With very special thanks and love to my parents, Elizabeth and Donald McKinley, their eyes always turned to plants, and my mother's, also, to history. And to my children, who serve me magic and beautiful chaos. To Nancy Miller, my wonderful editor, with whom I am so fortunate to have worked; Charlotte Sheedy, my agent, whom I deeply admire and thank for years of friendship; and Karen Shatzkin, whose support has been so critical. Thanks to Meredith Kaffel for her elbow grease and diligence.

I would not have been able to do the essential groundwork for this book without the support of a J. William Fulbright fellowship. I thank Walter Jackson of the Institute of International Education, and the former staff at USIS, Accra, especially Brooks Robinson and Robert Arbuckle, for their support and kindness during the grant period. The Frederick Lewis Allen Memorial Room at the Stephen A. Schwarzman Building of the New York Public Library provided a desk and many hours of quiet. Sarah Lawrence College provided a faculty grant for travel to the Vlisco archives in Helmond, Netherlands, and the Sarah Lawrence College Publications Fund provided monies for other research. Frans van Rood and Ruud

Sanders at Vlisco opened their doors to the company's extraordinary archives. Thanks to Fariha Chowdhury for fine assistance with research. Emily Robateau was a smart, tireless reader who shared a magical bit of Ghana with me while she worked on her own book. Margo Jefferson, Retha Powers, and Carolyn Ferrell helped with early drafts and always with cheer. Kati Torda was always ready to provide a Ghana fact, a translation, or cloth.

Andre Davis shared part of the journey. Nana-Ama Meri Danquah provided the first bit of backup vision when I doubted. Karen Hein and Sherry Bronfman offered inspiration and share my love of African blues. The historian Judith Byfield, who has written extensively about Nigeria and indigo, has been an inspiration, and her work means a great deal to me. Duncan Clarke shares my passion for indigo and has been a wonderful person to exchange ideas and knowledge with.

And finally thanks to the countless people in Ghana and elsewhere who opened their homes and cloth boxes, but especially to my dear Eurama, *Abusua*.

# BIBLIOGRAPHY

Barkley, Susan. *Adire: Indigo Cloth of Nigeria*. Catalog, Museum for Textiles, October 1980.

Beier, Ulli. *A Sea of Indigo*. Wuppertal, Germany: Edition Trickster/Peter Hammer Verlag, 1997.

Byfield, Judith A. *The Bluest Hands: A Social and Economic History of Women Dyers in Abeokuta (Nigeria), 1890–1940*. Portsmouth, N.H.: Heinemann, 2002.

Hartman, Saidiya. *Lose Your Mother: A Journey Along the Atlantic Slave Route*. New York: Farrar, Straus & Giroux, 2008.

Hollander, Stacy C. "Blue," *Folk Art* 29, no. 3 (Fall 2004).

Kriger, Colleen E. *Cloth in West African History*. New York: Altamira/Rowman & Littlefield, 2006.

Kroese, Dr. W. T. *The Origin of the Wax Block Prints on the Coast of West Africa*. Hengelo, Netherlands: N.V. Uitgeverij Smit, 1976.

Nast, Heidi J. *Concubines and Power*. Minneapolis: University of Minnesota Press, 2004.

Perbi, Akosua Adoma. *A History of Indigenous Slavery in Ghana from the 15th to the 19th Century*. Legon-Accra, Ghana: Sub-Saharan Publishers, 2004.

Polokoff, Claire. *Into Indigo*. Garden City, N.Y.: Anchor Books, 1980.

Shea, Philip James. *The Development of an Export Oriented Dyed Cloth Industry in Kano Emirate in the Nineteenth Century*. Ph.D. diss. Madison: University of Wisconsin, 1975.

Taussig, Michael. *What Color is the Sacred?* Chicago: University of Chicago Press, 1999.

van Koert, Robin. *Dutch Wax Design Technology from Helmond to West Africa: Uniwax and GTP in Post-Colonial Côte d'Ivoire and Ghana*. Eindhoven, Netherlands: Stichting Afrikaanse Dutch Wax, 2007.

Vaz, Kim Marie. *The Woman with the Artistic Brush: A Life History of Yoruba Batik Artist Nike Davies*. Armonk, N.Y.: M. E. Sharpe, 1995.

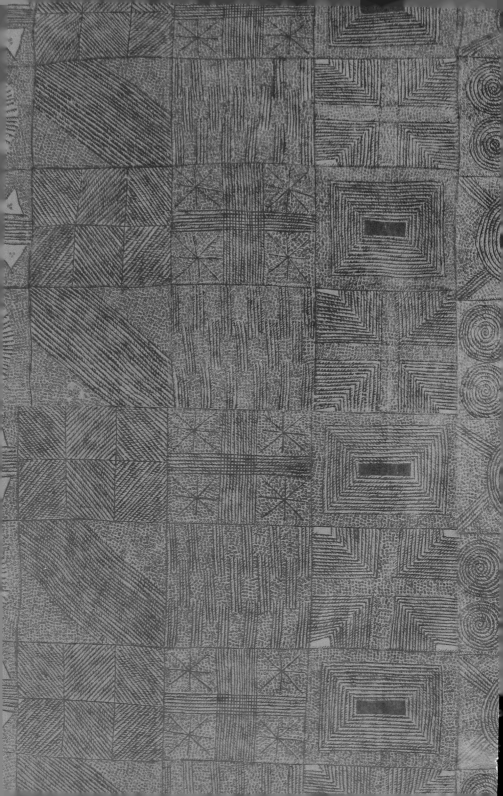